Electricity Requirements for a Digital Society

Walter S. Baer

Scott Hassell

Ben Vollaard

T0159563

Prepared for the
U.S. Department of Energy

RAND Science and Technology

RAND

The research described in this report was conducted by RAND Science and Technology for the U.S. Department of Energy.

Library of Congress Cataloging-in-Publication Data

Baer, Walter S.
　　Electricity requirements for a digital society / Walter S. Baer, Scott Hassell, Ben Vollaard.
　　　p. cm.
　　"MR-1617."
　　Includes bibliographical references.
　　ISBN 0-8330-3279-8
　　1. Telecommunications systems—Power supply. 2. Electric power consumption—United States—Forecasting. I. Hassell, Scott, 1974– II. Vollaard, Ben A., 1975– III.Title.

TK5102.5 .B296 2002
333.79'6—dc21

2002036757

Published 2002 by RAND
1700 Main Street, P.O. Box 2138, Santa Monica, CA 90407-2138
1200 South Hayes Street, Arlington, VA 22202-5050
201 North Craig Street, Suite 202, Pittsburgh, PA 15213
RAND URL: http://www.rand.org/
To order RAND documents or to obtain additional information, contact Distribution Services: Telephone: (310) 451-7002; Fax: (310) 451-6915; Email: order@rand.org

This report documents the results of a study conducted for the National Renewable Energy Laboratory (NREL) of the U.S. Department of Energy (DOE) on how the Internet and related information and communications technologies (ICTs) may influence future supply, demand, and delivery of electricity in the United States. The DOE needs a better understanding of the important factors driving the transition toward a digital society and the likely changes that it will bring about—both to make better estimates of future energy requirements and to inform planning for its long-term energy R&D portfolio.

Rather than attempt to make specific technology forecasts in a rapidly changing and highly uncertain environment, this study developed four different scenarios of ICT evolution over the 20-year period 2001–2021 and explored their implications for U.S. electricity requirements. The results are compared to the electricity use projections made by the DOE Energy Information Administration (EIA) and then discussed in relation to the R&D portfolio of the Office of Energy Efficiency and Renewable Energy (EERE).

RAND SCIENCE AND TECHNOLOGY

RAND is a nonprofit institution that helps improve policy and decisionmaking through research and analysis. RAND Science and Technology (S&T), one of RAND's research units, assists government and corporate decisionmakers in developing options to address challenges created by scientific innovation, rapid technological change, and world events. RAND S&T's research agenda is diverse. Its main areas of concentration are science and technology aspects of energy supply and use; environmental studies; transportation planning; space and aerospace issues; information infrastructure; biotechnology; and the federal R&D portfolio.

Inquiries regarding RAND Science and Technology may be directed to:

Steve Rattien
Director, RAND Science and Technology
RAND
1200 South Hayes Street
Arlington, VA 22202-5050
703-413-1100 x5219
www.rand.org/scitech

CONTENTS

TABLES

and with too much turbulence to permit technology forecasting, mapping, or assessment over 20 years.

Our four ICT scenarios make different assumptions about levels of ICT ownership and use, the growth of e-commerce and other ICT applications, and the principal ICT-related issues society must deal with. In brief:

- **Reference scenario.** This scenario describes a relatively straight-forward, "few surprises" extrapolation of current technology and application trends, leading to widespread societal use of ICTs and networked services, with an overall balance between centralized and decentralized control. Security, privacy, and other ICT-related problems persist, but U.S. society has achieved generally workable solutions for them.

- **Zaibatsu scenario.** In this scenario, large conglomerate corporations (known as *Zaibatsu* in Japan) own and operate the ICT (and electricity) infrastructures. They control e-commerce, ICT-intensive "intelligent transportation systems," and most other ICT applications. ICT usage is even higher in this centralized scenario than in the Reference scenario, and although the Zaibatsu and the federal government exercise strong economic and social controls, most Americans accept the Zaibatsu for the security and stability they have brought to society.

- **Cybertopia scenario.** In this scenario, there is equally high use and trust of networked ICT as in Zaibatsu, but control of the technology is more distributed, to individuals as well as large and small organizations. Tens of billions of embedded ICT devices linked by wireless networks have been deployed for public and private applications. Economic markets and consumer preferences largely determine individual use of ICT products and services, with light government regulation and modest subsidies for low-income and other targeted groups.

- **Net Insecurity scenario.** This scenario is less optimistic than the others. Persistent, unresolved security problems reduce public trust in and use of networked ICT applications and services. Large businesses, government agencies, and individuals who can afford to do so rely on highly secured private networks for information, communications, and transactions. Others mostly avoid interactive services and watch digital high-definition television displayed on large flat screens at home.

For each of these scenarios, we developed estimates of ICT-driven electricity use through 2021 and compared them with projections made by the U.S. Energy Information Administration (EIA) in its most recent *Annual Energy Outlook* (which we refer to as the *AEO 2002*).

The projections we made in this study consider three distinct kinds of ICT influence: (1) electricity consumption by ICT equipment, (2) changes in electricity use brought about by ICT-facilitated energy management systems (EMSs), and (3) implications for electricity usage of ICT-driven trends such as e-commerce and telework. Consumption by ICT equipment is the most direct and visible effect, but not necessarily the most important. Over time, ICT influences on energy management and on broader socioeconomic trends will likely have much more consequential effects on electricity and other energy use. However, they imply behavioral as well as technological changes and thus are much more difficult to estimate. This was a principal reason for developing several scenarios rather than making a single projection.

GROWTH IN ICT USE WILL ONLY MODESTLY INCREASE TOTAL ELECTRICITY USE

From the perspective of kilowatt-hours consumed, we found that very large increases in the number of digital devices over the next 20 years will have only modest effects on electricity demand. We looked for, but did not find, a set of plausible assumptions that might support another scenario, one with ICT networks, computers, and office equipment using 10 percent or more of the national electricity total by 2021. In none of our 2021 scenarios does this percentage exceed 5.5 percent.

All four of our scenarios show lower total power consumption in 2021 than was projected in the *AEO 2002*, ranging from 3 percent less in Net Insecurity to 11 percent less in Cybertopia. This difference stems principally from our baseline 2001 estimates for power use by computer, office, and network ICT equipment being more than 75 terawatt-hours (TWh), or 45 percent, below those in the *AEO 2002*.

The difference widens to more than 200 TWh when projected forward to 2021.

For 2021, our electricity use projections, compared to those extrapolated from the *AEO 2002*, are higher for the residential sector and lower for the commercial and industrial sectors. In our Reference scenario, the 2021 projected total for all three sectors is 4,630 TWh, which is 7 percent below the *AEO 2002* projection. EMSs in buildings and telework are responsible for the greatest electricity savings, with digital industrial process controls and e-commerce also making substantial contributions.

Of the scenarios, Net Insecurity uses the most electricity, primarily because this scenario's loss of trust in public networks results in lower power savings from EMSs, e-commerce, and telework. In contrast, Cybertopia's much higher use of EMSs, e-commerce, and telework brings power savings that are 400 TWh (9 percent) greater than those of Net Insecurity and 570 TWh (11 percent) greater than those of the *AEO 2002* projection. The relatively narrow range of 400 TWh between our lowest and highest projections for power use in 2021 reflects our analysis that ICT represents a factor of roughly 5 to 6 percent in explaining U.S. total electricity consumption. Of course, all these projections are rough estimates based on incomplete data and a large number of assumptions about how the future will unfold.

For the important category of computer, office, and network ICT equipment, the projections indicate relatively modest increases in power consumption over the 20-year period. Our 2001 estimate of 118 TWh represents 3.4 percent of total electricity use, which is far below some earlier estimates but consistent with recent data. Looking forward, greater power demands from larger numbers of more powerful digital devices will be moderated by greater use of more electricity-efficient components, low-power embedded devices, and wireless equipment and networks.

Our analysis also led to additional findings that appear robust across the scenarios:

- Telework and ICT-facilitated energy management can have large effects on electricity consumption;

- Expanded use of both digital process controls in manufacturing and business-to-business e-commerce brings power savings that while not as large as those for telework and EMS are more consistent among scenarios with quite different assumptions;

- Business-to-consumer e-commerce has smaller effects on overall electricity consumption;

- The power-saving effects of EMSs in the residential sector depend less on ICT advances than on consumers' behavioral response to time-of-use or real-time pricing;

- Telework increases electricity consumption in the residential sector while lowering it in the commercial and industrial sectors, the net effect depending both on the number of teleworkers and the average number of days spent teleworking.

THE ELECTRICITY SYSTEM NEEDS TO FOCUS ON HIGHER POWER QUALITY AND RELIABILITY

In addition to making quantitative projections of electricity use, our analysis identified four important, cross-cutting energy supply issues:

- Assurance of power quality for very large numbers of digital devices;

- Use of ICT to improve grid reliability and operations;

- Use of ICT to support distributed generation and storage;

- Reduction of the vulnerability of the ICT and electricity infrastructures.

Previous debate has focused largely on the issue of how much electricity will be needed to power the Internet and related ICT equipment. Our analysis, however, concludes that meeting the increased demand for higher power quality and reliability (PQR) will be a more important issue for a digital society. We thus recommend that the Office of Energy Efficiency and Renewable Energy (EERE) explicitly include the goal of improving power quality in its strategic plan, as well as in appropriate R&D and technology programs.

A related conclusion: The electricity supply and distribution systems necessary to support a digital society will increasingly rely on power electronics and other ICT developments for improved power measurement, monitoring, and control. These ICT advances are essential to improving PQR for digital loads, increasing grid reliability, enabling the growth of distributed energy resources, and making electricity and ICT infrastructures more robust and resilient.

POLICY IMPLICATIONS: EXPANDED USE OF R&D TO DEVELOP ICTs AND DEPLOY THEM IN THE ELECTRICITY SYSTEM

EERE may need to pay greater attention to accelerating the development of ICTs and their deployment in the U.S. electric power system. Our scenarios emphasize the importance of bringing the results of R&D into commercial practice to support the increased future demands of digital loads, especially in the two high-ICT-use, Zaibatsu and Cybertopia scenarios. In-time deployment of ICT in the electricity infrastructure depends on R&D success in reducing costs as well as in increasing performance. While EERE supports a number of projects in these areas, most of the relevant R&D is industry funded and has been under financial pressure as the industry restructures. Electricity industry restructuring may well lead to underinvestment in R&D and infrastructure improvements, although we cannot conclude that such possible market failures will seriously constrain ICT growth.

We recommend that EERE assess the goals, schedules, obstacles, and likely outcomes of current government and industry R&D programs in such areas as

- Power electronics for transmission and distribution (T&D);
- Power sources for very small, wireless digital devices;
- Energy storage for high PQR applications;
- Self-healing microgrids and T&D networks.

If the analysis finds evidence for underinvestment, or for mismatches between likely availability and need, a good case can be made for

PQR	power quality and reliability
R&D	research and development
RTP	real-time pricing
S&T	Science and Technology
SCADA	Supervisory Control and Data Acquisition
SCM	supply chain management
SMES	superconducting magnetic energy storage
SSL	secure socket link
T&D	transmission and distribution
Tbps	Terabits per second
TOU	time of use
TWh	Terawatt-hours
2G, 3G, 4G	2nd, 3rd, 4th generation
VAT	Value-Added Tax
VMT	vehicle miles traveled
WAN	wide area network
XML	Extensible Markup Language

Chapter One

INTRODUCTION

1.1 INFORMATION AND COMMUNICATIONS TECHNOLOGIES AND ENERGY IN A DIGITAL SOCIETY

Many Americans believe that the United States is moving steadily toward a digital society, although few would agree on precisely what this term means. To some, a digital society implies growing reliance on networked information and communications technologies (ICTs), with more and more people using the Internet and such other ICTs as cell phones, digital video recorders, digital music players and, of course, personal computers (PCs). To others, such a society suggests changes in the structure and operation of the economy that emphasize higher productivity, quicker obsolescence of capital goods and human skills, the use of customized processes to make better products at lower cost, and the growth of ICT-intensive businesses such as electronic commerce (e-commerce).[1] To still others, a digital society is characterized by significant changes in how individuals spend their time and relate to other people;[2] examples could include "teleworking" from home instead of commuting to an office, organizing a social event by electronic mail (email) rather than by telephone or

---

[1] The emergence of a "digital economy" in the United States and other industrialized countries is now the topic of a large and growing literature, upon which this study draws. See, for example, Margeherio et al., 1998; U.S. Department of Commerce, 2000; OECD, 1999; Brynjolfsson and Kahin, 2000; and Jorgenson and Stiroh, 2001.

[2] A good discussion of and links to the literature on social impacts of ITC can be found at UCLA professor Philip Agre's Website, http://dlis.gseis.ucla.edu/people/pagre/rre.html. For a European perspective, see Ducatel, Webster, and Herrmann, 2000.

letter, and playing bridge with a partner over the Internet instead of entertaining friends or watching television at home.

Whether the focus is on technology, the economy, or society at large, it is widely accepted that ICTs will have profound effects on individuals and organizations over the next two decades. But there is as yet little agreement about what these effects imply for the use of electricity and other forms of energy in the United States. Mark Mills and Peter Huber (Mills, 1999; Huber and Mills, 1999; and Huber, 2000), whose estimates have been widely reported in the press and in congressional testimony, argue that the Internet and related ICT equipment consumed some 8 percent of U.S electric power in 1998 and will require a much larger share in the future. However, researchers at Lawrence Berkeley National Laboratory and Arthur D. Little, Inc., who conducted more-detailed studies (Koomey et al., 1999; Koomey, 2000; and Roth, Goldstein, and Kleinman, 2002) than did Mills and Huber conclude that Mills and Huber's estimates are highly overstated and that computer, office, and network ICT equipment accounted for only about 3 percent of U.S. power consumption in 1999/2000.[3] Other analysts who challenge the Mills and Huber power growth assumptions believe that growing use of ICTs will likely reduce U.S. electricity intensity in the future.[4]

1.2 REPORT OBJECTIVES, SCOPE, AND ORGANIZATION

The study's principal goal was to build a broad framework for analyzing the relationships among ICTs, their likely economic and social consequences, and future energy requirements. We constructed a series of plausible scenarios for ICT growth and use from 2001 to 2021 through which to identify important driving factors and to distinguish likely trends and developments from those that are more speculative or highly uncertain. In this approach, technical and nontechnical factors are interwoven. For instance, in analyzing the implications of digital technology for energy management in the home, one must estimate both the technologies that will be available and affordable (e.g., digital electricity meters and appliances con-

---

[3]Also see Hayes, 2001.

[4]For example, see Romm, Rosenfeld, and Herrmann, 1999.

nected to home networks), *and* the ways in which consumers will respond to developments (e.g., electricity prices that vary by time of day or by the overall level of demand).

Our report tries to indicate explicitly what restrictions and assumptions underlie the scenarios, and where the greatest questions and uncertainties remain. This point is important for understanding not only the analysis itself, but also the policy implications that can reasonably be drawn from the analysis. For example, while the Internet obviously has global scope and reach, this report deliberately emphasizes ICT developments and implications in the United States. Thus, its findings and conclusions do not necessarily apply to countries other than the United States. The report also focuses on ICT implications for electricity, giving rather limited attention to the implications for oil, natural gas, and other fuels.

Chapter Two of this report discusses the approach, methodology, and data sources we used to generate our 20-year ICT scenarios, which are then described in Chapter Three. Chapter Four presents quantitative projections of U.S. electricity consumption for each scenario from 2001 through 2021; Chapter Five discusses the implications of the scenarios for such electricity supply issues as power quality and reliability, evolution of the transmission and distribution grid, distributed energy resources, and infrastructure vulnerabilities. Chapter Six contains our findings and policy recommendations. Further details about the scenarios and electricity use projections are provided in two appendices.

Chapter Two

APPROACH AND METHODOLOGY

2.1 WHY CREATE SCENARIOS?

To assess how information and communications technologies (ICTs) will affect electric power over the next 20 years, one must estimate what ICT developments will occur and what their effects are likely to be. While this clearly is not an easy task, there are various approaches, or methodologies, that can be employed as aids: technology forecasts, roadmaps, assessments, and scenarios.

The first three of these approaches usually focus on a technological end point, range, or path. A technology *forecast* is, as the term suggests, a prediction about the characteristics of a particular technology at a particular future time (Martino, 1978, pp. 1–2). The forecast may be a point estimate or an estimated range incorporating the level of uncertainty associated with the prediction. A technology *roadmap* depicts the key scientific and technical advances needed to reach a desired end state, or "destination."[1] A technological *assessment* is principally concerned with "evaluating the social consequences of [a] technological change" (Pool, 1983, p. 2). Like technology forecasts, roadmaps and assessments generally treat uncertainty as an excursion around a preferred path or destination.

In contrast, a *scenario* includes uncertainty as an essential feature of the exploration. It develops both the technical and nontechnical characteristics of "an alternative future plus a description of the path

---

[1]Technology roadmaps relevant to this study include EPRI, 1999a; and Info-Communications Development Authority of Singapore, 2000.

that goes from today to that future" (Dewar, 2002), its goal being to provide a self-consistent future world with a credible narrative leading to a plausible end point. Together, several scenarios span a space that is considered likely to contain the actual future state, although any individual scenario is by itself unlikely to be realized.

We chose the scenario approach because we believe changes in ICTs are happening too fast and with too much turbulence to permit forecasting, mapping, or assessment over a 20-year period. In the words of a recent National Research Committee report on the future of the Internet, "The middle of a revolution is a difficult point from which to gauge long-term outcomes" (Computer Science and Telecommunications Board, 2001a, p. 2). By offering several plausible alternative paths and end points, scenarios can aid policymakers by challenging assumptions, revealing possible gaps in planning, and suggesting adaptive or hedging strategies for contingency planning and research and development (R&D) programs.[2]

2.2 APPROACH TO DEVELOPING ICT SCENARIOS

In constructing the ICT scenarios, we followed a process that RAND has used for other scenario-building exercises. In our case, it involved the following six steps:

- Review ICT trends and developments;
- Review recently published scenarios and planning documents;
- Characterize current and future ICT applications;
- Interview ICT and other experts to identify important technical and nontechnical driving factors;
- Identify likely and possible implications of ICT developments;
- Synthesize the results into a small number of scenarios that depict different ICT development paths and societal outcomes.

---

[2]Beginning in the late 1960s, Royal Dutch/Shell pioneered the use of scenarios in these ways for business planning. For accounts of the Royal Dutch/Shell experience, see Wack, 1985; Schwartz, 1991; and Van der Heijden, 1996. Also see Smil, 2000.

When considering technology trends, it is useful to look back at least as far as one intends to look forward. Consequently, we reviewed ICT studies from the late 1970s through the present that were conducted by the National Research Council, the Office of Technology Assessment, the Aspen Institute, and others.[3] Recent scenarios of interest included, among others, those created for the Central Intelligence Agency (National Intelligence Council, 2000), the U.S. Air Force (Air University, 1995), the European Commission (Information Society Technologies Advisory Group, 2001; and Botterman et al., 2001), the Millennium Project of the American Council for the United Nations University (Glenn and Gordon, 2000), and the Department of Energy (DOE) Interlaboratory Working Group (2000). A number of recent trade books by ICT stakeholders also provided popular and often insightful accounts of prospective ICT developments.[4]

To be useful to corporate decisionmakers or government policymakers, scenarios must be interesting, relevant, and few. If there are many scenarios dealing with multiple outcomes or possibilities, the situation quickly becomes unmanageable and the scenarios therefore unhelpful. "Never more than four" is a consistent theme among successful scenario builders (Wack, 1985b). As a consequence, we had to sift through a large number of possible influences on ICT evolution to find one or two drivers to form the framework for very different but self-consistent future paths and end states.

2.3 ICT DRIVING FACTORS

A great many technical and nontechnical factors interact in influencing the path and pace of movement toward a digital society:

* Innovations in ICT products and services, which make them better, cheaper, and easier to use;

---

[3]Examples include reports from the Computer Science and Telecommunications Board, 2001a, 2001b, 1997, 1996, 1995, 1994, and 1988; Anderson et al., 2000; Hundley et al., 2000; Kahan, 1993; and Robinson, 1978.

[4]See, for example, Negroponte, 1995; Gates, Myhrvold, and Rinearson, 1996; Mitchell, 1997; Dertouzos, 1998; Norman, 1998; and Kurzweil, 1998. A more complete list of recent trade books about digital technology can be found at http://www.nytimes.com/books/specials/digital.html (last accessed August 30, 2002).

- Development of new and/or better ICT network applications;

- Investments in ICT and related infrastructure;

- Demand for ICT products, services, and applications, which drives their adoption and diffusion rates;

- Industry and market structures for ICT products, services, and applications;

- Extent of regulation or other government controls;

- Public trust and confidence in ICT networks, services, and applications;

- Overall economic, political, social, and security environment.

An essential characteristic of a digital society is near-universal access to and pervasive use of ICT equipment, services, and networks in all ordinary pursuits and venues: working, learning, traveling, doing routine chores, interacting with friends and family, and relaxing at home. Widespread availability and use of digital technologies seem far more important than does the nature of the technologies themselves. In fact, the closer the United States moves toward a digital society, the more embedded and invisible the technologies become. This is a major theme in most of the literature cited earlier, just as it was in the interviews with experts and brainstorming sessions we conducted during this project.

As a result, we selected ICT level of use as the first of two principal drivers of the scenarios. We also discovered from our literature search and personal discussions that there is a strong correlation between use and trust—a discovery that, in hindsight, should not have been very surprising. Individuals and institutions must have trust in networked ICT products and services before they will use them (or permit them to be used by others in their organization) for important functions. The link between trust and use has been observed consistently in the adoption of ICTs ranging from telephone answering machines to automatic teller machines, and today this link regulates the expansion of e-commerce and other Internet applications.[5]

---

[5]The Computer Science and Telecommunications Board (1999, p. 13) provides a good definition of trust in a networked information system (NIS): a "trustworthy NIS does

Society's approach to regulating or controlling networked ICTs constitutes the second principal driver of the scenarios. Specifically, we distinguish centralized economic, governmental, and social controls from those that are more decentralized or distributed. Monopoly provision of goods and services, rules set by large organizations, and strong federal laws embody centralized controls—compared to the decentralized controls represented by (economically efficient) markets for goods and services, policies set by small organizations, and local government regulation. We chose the locus of control as a scenario driver partly because it is important for both ICT and energy systems, but more because centralized controls and decentralized controls lead to quite different evolutionary paths toward a digital society.

2.4 DATA, ASSUMPTIONS, AND UNCERTAINITIES IN THE SCENARIOS

Baseline data for the scenarios and analysis were taken from many government and private sources (cited here and in the chapters that follow). Population, demographic, and household data are from the 2000 U.S. Census (2001a); estimates of the size and scope of the U.S. "digital economy" are primarily from recent Department of Commerce documents (Margeherio et al., 1998; and U.S. Department of Commerce, 2000). Electricity and related energy data are from the Energy Information Administration (2001)—specifically, the *Annual Energy Outlook 2002 with Projections to 2020,* which we refer to in this report as the *AEO 2002*—and from EPRI[6] and other industry sources. Our 2001 estimates of U.S. stocks and use of computers and other ICT equipment and services are based on Census data; on studies/surveys conducted by Lawrence Berkeley National Laboratory,[7] Arthur D. Little, Inc. (Roth, Goldstein, and Kleinman, 2002), the Pew Internet and American Life Project (2002), and the UCLA Center for Communication Policy (2001); and on estimates from a variety of industry experts, industry associations, and trade journals.

---

what people expect it to do—and not something else—despite environmental disruption, human user and operator errors, and attacks by hostile parties."

[6]Formerly the Electric Power Research Institute.

[7]Chapter Four provides the relevant references.

The scenario projections through 2021 are entirely our own responsibility, but they were aided by and compared with projections in the *AEO 2002* and in shorter-term industry forecasts.[8] The assumptions underlying the scenarios are described in the following chapter and in greater detail in Appendix A. Uncertainties are largely built into the scenario structure—for example, each scenario makes its own assumptions about consumers' use of e-commerce two decades from now. Technology availability thus leads to very different consequences in different scenarios.

We have tried to make the assumptions in the scenarios as explicit and transparent as possible; but, of course, many additional details and possibilities are left out. We do not, for example, examine the consequences of "high" or "low" energy prices in future years, as does the *AEO 2002*. Nor do we estimate the effects of differing assumptions about future economic growth or lifestyle that are not ICT related. Perhaps most important, our scenarios do not include major international events such as wars, long-term disruptions of oil or gas supplies, or environmental catastrophes. Our focus is on ICT-driven effects on the U.S. economy and society, although we do recognize that national security and political drivers can easily overwhelm results stemming from technological change.

Our ICT scenarios complement scenarios being created elsewhere to explore international and other driving factors, all of which will contribute to the overall planning efforts of the Office of Energy Efficiency and Renewable Energy (EERE) and DOE. They are intended to help decisionmakers who are thinking about the uncertainties inherent in technology and energy projections and considering what actions can be taken now as possible hedges against the adverse consequences of future surprises.

---

[8]Good starting places for seeking such industry forecasts are Cyberatlas, at http://cyberatlas.internet.com, and eMarketer, at http://www.emarketer.com. Another useful forecast through 2010 is in Sanchez et al., 1998.

Chapter Three

INFORMATION AND COMMUNICATIONS
TECHNOLOGY SCENARIOS

3.1 OVERVIEW OF SCENARIOS

As stated in Chapter Two, the principal drivers of our 20-year (2001–2021) scenarios are the overall use of and trust in information and communications technologies (ICTs), and the relative emphasis on centralized versus distributed ICT control. We first developed one scenario for the first five years, 2001 through 2006, that is common to all of the 20-year scenarios. This common scenario depicts a fairly straight-line extrapolation of current technical, demographic, and behavioral trends, without significant surprises.

Figure 3.1 shows schematically the path from 2001 to 2006 within a two-by-two matrix whose vertical and horizontal axes are, respectively, the level of ICT use and trust, and the locus of ICT control. Note that overall ICT usage in 2006 is at the lower edge of the matrix, whereas 2001 usage sits below the matrix. The figure essentially establishes 2006 as the base for discussing subsequent developments and represents our view that ICT usage will increase substantially from 2001 to 2006 in all plausible scenarios. We assume that the locus of control will move only slightly toward decentralization during this first five-year period.

With 2006 as the divergence point, Figure 3.2 shows the relationship between the 2006 base and the 2021 end points for the four scenarios. The "Reference" scenario shown essentially continues along the path of the first five years, moving steadily upward in usage and modestly toward further decentralization over the 15 years from 2006

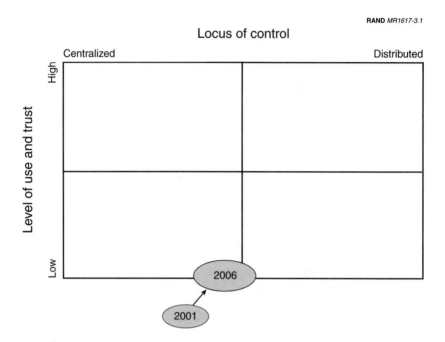

Figure 3.1—Common 2001–2006 Scenario

to 2021. The second scenario, "Zaibatsu," depicts even higher ICT usage, with highly centralized control. The third scenario, "Cyber-topia," shows ICT usage equally as high as that of Zaibatsu, but with control largely decentralized. The fourth, "Net Insecurity," exhibits less overall ICT usage in 2021 compared to the other three (although more than the 2006 base), with more centralized than decentralized controls.

All of the scenarios are described and discussed further in the remainder of this chapter; their underlying assumptions are presented in greater detail in Appendix A.

3.2 COMMON 2001–2006 SCENARIO

The first five years see continuing advances in ICTs and both a broadening and a deepening of ICT use in the United States. Moore's Law remains fully in force in this common scenario, doubling the

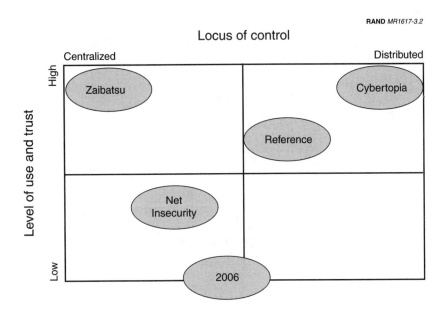

Figure 3.2—Relationship of 2021 Scenarios to 2006 Base

number of electronic components on a semiconductor chip every 18 to 24 months and making ICT products and systems ever faster, better, and cheaper. Optical fiber bandwidth and computer memory show even more-rapid gains. Steady progress continues in ICT hardware and software technologies, such as optical communication networks, voice recognition, biometrics, and micro-electromechanical systems (MEMS). And by 2006, the number of "information appliances" and other specialized devices—most of them wireless—exceeds the number of PCs connected to the Internet.

3.2.1 Ownership and Use of ICT Devices

Table 3.1 summarizes our projected trends in ownership and use of digital ICT devices between 2001 and 2006. Wireless growth outstrips wired network growth, resulting in more than two-thirds of U.S. adults having cell phones and/or personal digital assistants (PDAs) by 2006 (although this percentage is still below that of wireless users in Scandinavia and some other countries). The common scenario as-

Table 3.1

**Projected Trends in Ownership and Use of ICT Devices,
2001–2006**

	Percentage	
	2001	2006
Households with telephone service	94	95
Adults with cell phone/PDA	40	70
Adults using Net	70	90
Households with computer	52	80
Households with Net access	35	70
Households with broadband Net access	9	30
Households with cable or satellite TV	75	80
Households with digital TV receiver	<1	8
Households with broadband home network	3	20
Households with networked EMS	<1	10

sumes that delays in building out third-generation wireless networks translate to relatively few users having broadband wireless access to the Internet from home at data speeds greater than 256 kilobits per second (kbps).[1] However, broadband wireless data access is more generally available in airports, hotels, cafes, offices, and other commercial buildings.

By 2006, 90 percent of U.S. adults actively use the Internet (known simply as "the Net") at home, work, or school. Seventy percent of households have Net access; 30 percent have broadband access from home above 256 kbps, primarily via the legacy coaxial cable and copper networks.[2] Fiber-to-the-home is still a rarity. In rural areas,

---

[1]The 256 kbps represents a current (2002) perspective of "broadband" Internet access, mostly available through cable modem or telephone digital subscriber line service. In future years, *broadband* will undoubtedly be redefined to require data speeds of megabits or gigabits per second.

[2]The increase in broadband households from 9 percent in 2001 to 30 percent in 2006 implies a compound annual growth rate of 27 percent, which is considerably below the 50 to 100 percent annual growth in digital subscriber line and cable modem connections observed from 1997 to 2001. We project that broadband growth will be lower from 2001 to 2006 due to the bursting of the dot.com bubble, the economic recession that began in 2001, and steep reductions in capital expenditures by the major telephone and cable providers. Our projections also are net of customers discontinuing broadband service, which is known as "churn."

satellites permit data downloading from the Net at broadband speeds, but most data links upstream from homes remain at speeds below 128 kbps.

Fewer than 10 percent of households have purchased a digital TV receiver by 2006, although nearly half have set-top digital boxes installed to receive digital television signals from cable or satellite. Most households own several digital game consoles, digital music players, digital video cameras, digital versatile disk (DVD) players, and digital video recording devices. Broadband "smart home" networks are important sales features in upscale new houses, condominiums, and apartments; overall, some 20 percent of residences have wired or wireless home networks in 2006. Home networks are principally used for security and child monitoring, as well as for interconnecting computer, office, and entertainment devices. New refrigerators and other major appliances often come with addressable chips and are advertised as "home network ready," but at this point relatively few households actually use the networking features. Similarly, use of home networks for energy management systems (EMSs) has been slow to take off, although digital utility meters and time-of-use pricing are beginning to penetrate the residential market.

3.2.2 E-Commerce and Other ICT Applications

Despite the Internet bubble of the late 1990s and the dot.com disasters that followed, business-to-business (B2B) e-commerce continues to improve and extend its reach. By 2006, the vast majority of firms routinely use intranets and/or the Net for online procurement, supply chain management, customer service, banking and related treasury functions, and financial communications. Payments for B2B transactions have become largely automated. Large firms conduct much of their routine business online and encourage their employees to focus on face-to-face contacts among colleagues, suppliers, and customers for important matters.

Although most of the business-to-consumer (B2C) e-commerce startups fold in the 2001–2002 recession, overall B2C keeps growing throughout the downturn and rebounds strongly afterward. By 2006, 60 percent of U.S. adults purchase some goods and services on the Net (up from 35 percent in 2001), and nearly half have participated in one or more online auctions. An appreciable share of consumer travel, banking, and other financial transactions is conducted online. The spread of smart credit and debit cards with digital signatures has improved online security enough that customer complaints and disputes are at about the same level for online as for conventional transactions. Consumers routinely use software agents to compare prices and other features among competing online vendors and to recommend specific purchases, but relatively few people let agents complete their transactions: they prefer to make final buying decisions themselves.

Teleworking from home expands nearly 50 percent, going from 17 million (9 percent of the adult work force) in 2001 to 25 million (13 percent of the adult work force) in 2006.[3] However, most teleworkers work only part-time at home, spending the majority of their work week at an office. Many other ICT applications that were in development or used only by early adopters in 2001 have moved further into the mainstream by 2006. For example:

- Movie theaters are converting from film images to high-definition digital formats;

- Theme parks have installed many more high-definition virtual environments;

- Most college students and one-third of working adults participate in some distance learning classes over the Net;

- Smart, miniaturized defibrillators, insulin pumps, and other medical devices are now routinely implanted in patients;

- Medical monitoring over the Net is offered to patients with smart implants, the elderly, and others with chronic conditions;

- Telemedicine is now more widely available in rural and urban areas but is used primarily for physician consults rather than primary patient care;

---

[3]The estimate of 17 million teleworkers in 2001 comes from Nilles, 2000. The Institute for the Study of Distributed Work (ISDW) at the University of California at Berkeley estimates a somewhat lower figure. The difference is likely due to different definitions of teleworking and different survey methods (Charles Grantham, ISDW, private communication, 2002).

- Nearly all commercial vehicles and more than half of new cars have global positioning system (GPS) and wireless navigation, safety, and security systems;

- New California vehicle license plates include a permanently installed, addressable "smart chip" for theft prevention and toll collection, among other applications;

- Networked environmental sensors to monitor air, water, and soil conditions are becoming common.

3.2.3 ICT Issues in 2006

The economic, social, and political issues surrounding ICTs in 2006 look remarkably like those of 2001. Although rhetoric over the "digital divide" has somewhat subsided, 30 percent of U.S. households are still unconnected to the Net, and the political debate now includes efforts to provide subsidized broadband access to low-income households. Many privacy and intellectual property rights issues also remain unresolved.

Security on the Net is clearly the number-one policy concern in 2006. Driven in large part by the terrorist attacks of 2001, strong new laws against cybercrime have been enacted, and hardware, software, and information providers have invested heavily in upgrading infrastructure security. Digital signatures with biometric identification keep fraud and other commercial cybercrime within acceptable limits, although identity theft (believed to come primarily from perpetrators outside the United States) remains a problem. Because of concerns about cybercrime, prison inmates no longer receive training in programming or other ICT skills.

However, new vulnerabilities appear with each new generation of ICT technology, and new computer viruses and other malicious codes continuously challenge Net operators and users. Although firewalls are now mandated for every broadband Net connection, a survey in 2005 found that less than half of home broadband users had successfully installed the latest security patches. The growing numbers of always-connected home computers are increasingly attractive targets for hackers and criminals. Many fear that security on the Net will not keep pace with attackers' new capabilities. Still, Net usage is growing strongly, and business, government, and consumer users rely more heavily on networked communications, information, and transactions in 2006 than ever before.

3.3 REFERENCE SCENARIO

As shown in Figure 3.3, the Reference scenario basically continues the 2001–2006 trends over the next 15 years. This vision of 2021 portrays an economy and society strongly linked with and dependent on ICTs. Nearly all individuals and organizations use ICT devices and network services in their daily lives with a high level of trust and confidence.

In terms of technology, smart embedded devices controlled by voice commands, complex software agents, biometric identification,

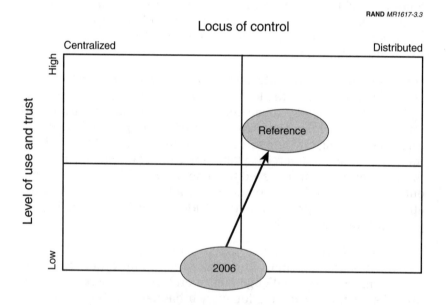

Figure 3.3—Reference Scenario Progression from 2006

videophones, and MEMS devices are in common use.[4] After more than 60 years of intensive R&D, voice recognition and natural language processing are finally cheap and reliable enough that humans can routinely operate machines by speaking to them (although traditional tactile controls usually complement voice when human judgment is important, as in driving). Voice recognition is especially important in facilitating the rapid growth of portable and embedded ICT devices without keypads or touch screen controls. By 2021, literally billions of smart portable and embedded devices are in use and have displaced general purpose computers for many Net applications.

3.3.1 Ownership and Use of ICT Devices

A large majority of Americans have both wireless and wired access to the Net at home, at work, and at school, and while traveling (Table 3.2). Wireless ICT devices have become small and cheap enough to be embedded into clothing, jewelry, and fashion accessories. Digital video entertainment has been technically integrated with other Net services and is mostly carried over fiber optic facilities, although remnants of legacy cable and copper-wire telephone networks still survive. By 2021, 75 percent of households are served by fiber, either directly to the home or to the utility access point nearest the home.[5] In rural areas, two-way broadband services are generally available via satellite and terrestrial wireless. Ninety percent of residences have broadband internal networks, most with energy management software linked to real-time prices for electricity and gas. However, actual consumer use of these systems to regulate energy consumption from heating, lighting, air conditioning, and appliances varies widely.

---

[4]It is also important to note the technologies that this scenario assumes are still in R&D or the early stages of commercial introduction in 2021 and thus not yet in common use. They include, among others, quantum computing, true nanotechnology (as opposed to MEMS), room temperature superconductors, refreshable "digital paper," and direct chip-to-brain implants in humans. These assumptions are clearly our judgment calls, but we believe they are supported by the fact that these breakthroughs require changes in industrial processes and human behavior that usually take two decades or more to move from R&D to widespread adoption. For a discussion of past examples, see Rogers, 1986.

[5]Running fiber to the nearest access point is known as fiber-to-the-curb (FTTC), as opposed to fiber-to-the-home (FTTH).

Table 3.2

ICT Ownership and Use, Reference Scenario

	Percentage	
	2006	2021
Adults with cell phone/PDA	70	90
Households with Net access	70	92
Households with broadband Net access	30	90
Households with multichannel TV	80	95
Households with fiber to the curb or home	<5	75
Households with digital TV receiver	8	95
Households with broadband home network	20	90
Households with networked EMS	10	70

3.3.2 E-Commerce and Other ICT Applications

B2B transactions primarily occur on the Net, and consumers make heavy use of B2C e-commerce, but retail stores still flourish. Software agents conduct most online transactions independently, checking with their human principals only as needed. Telework has grown steadily, both in number of adults and in average time spent tele-working. By 2021, 40 million people, constituting 18 percent of the adult work force, telework at least part-time.

Other ICT applications important to the economy and society of 2021 are as follows:

- Videoconferencing on the Net is widely used in both business and general communication;

- Multimedia entertainment in theaters and theme parks is highly realistic, approaching early 21st century concepts of "virtual reality," but it is still too expensive for most people at home;

- Online distance learning is fully integrated with on-site classes at all levels from elementary school to adult learning;

- MEMS implants remotely monitored on the Net are routine for many chronic medical conditions;

- Patients routinely perform diagnostic tests at home and call up medical information on the Net before seeking treatment, and telemedicine complements face-to-face medical visits;

- All post-2012 vehicles have embedded systems for identification, safety, location, toll payments, and other applications;

- Commercial and industrial facilities make extensive use of embedded networked sensors for heating, ventilating, and air conditioning (HVAC), lighting, and process controls;

- Environmental regulations require networked sensors at all large industrial and commercial sites for air and water monitoring and effluent control.

3.3.3   ICT Issues in 2021

ICT problems and issues persist in the Reference scenario, but U.S. society has achieved generally workable solutions for them. Both proprietary and open software standards thrive and compete against each other, and although some 15 million adults are still unconnected to the Net, the digital divide is no longer considered a major societal issue. (Access issues do remain prominent in developing countries, however.)

Security problems still affect the Net and related ICT services but are kept under control by a combination of technology and strictly enforced laws and regulations. All networked computers and devices must meet current security standards before they can be connected to the Net. Net traffic is routinely encrypted, and most public spaces (i.e., physical space, as opposed to cyberspace) are monitored by video cameras. Still, both public and private authorities wage constant battles to keep e-fraud and other cybercrime within acceptable limits. Embedded smart tags on vehicles have cut auto theft substantially since 2012. Biometric databases have become indispensable tools against cybercrime and are used extensively to monitor Net usage. And many states have been able to reduce their prison populations by enforcing house arrest with remote ICT monitoring.

Such security measures have necessarily reduced the "privacy sphere" for people outside their residences. Individuals, and society in general, have lower privacy expectations in 2021 than they did in

2006 (or 2001). Nevertheless, most people accept reduced privacy away from home as a satisfactory price to pay for the many benefits of ICTs in this increasingly digital society.

3.4 ZAIBATSU SCENARIO

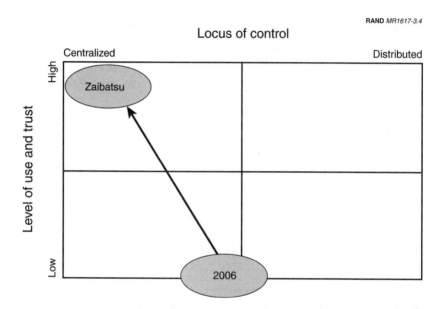

Figure 3.4—Zaibatsu Scenario Progression from 2006

In the Zaibatsu scenario, shown in Figure 3.4, large conglomerate corporations own and operate the information and communications infrastructure (along with the electricity and other infrastructures), and control e-commerce and most other ICT applications. Thus the label of "Zaibatsu"—the name given to their 20th century counterparts in Japan.

The path toward Zaibatsu begins in the second half of the first decade of the 21st century with the evident failure of deregulation in communications, energy, transportation, and financial services, and the recognized need for vastly increased protection of essential infrastructures after devastating terrorist attacks over several years.

New laws are passed (and upheld by the Supreme Court) that encourage both vertical and horizontal integration and provide for strong federal regulation (or re-regulation) of infrastructure and essential services. Industry consolidation quickly follows, and by 2010 the nation's infrastructures are owned and operated by eight very large firms with interlocking interests in multiple economic sectors. Within a few more years, each Zaibatsu has a well-established position in information hardware and software, entertainment, education, and health care, as well as in communication services, financial services, energy, transportation, and water. The Zaibatsu both cooperate and compete among themselves, under federal government supervision.

3.4.1 ICT Applications and Usage

Large infrastructure and R&D investments by the Zaibatsu over more than a decade result in more ICT use (Table 3.3) than occurs in the Reference scenario. To spur usage, the Zaibatsu essentially give everyone a "free" Net account providing basic voice and text communications, access to government information and services, and access to advertiser-supported video and other content. Users pay monthly or by usage for other services. Subscribers can choose equipment, content, and services from anyone connected to the Net, but each Zaibatsu offers substantial incentives to use its own affiliated suppliers.

Table 3.3

ICT Ownership and Use, Zaibatsu Scenario

	Percentage	
	2006	2021
Adults with cell phone/PDA	70	85
Households with Net access	70	98
Households with broadband Net access	30	96
Households with multichannel TV	80	95
Households with fiber to the curb or home	<5	85
Households with digital TV receiver	8	98
Households with broadband home network	20	95
Households with networked EMS	10	80

While ICT technological development does not differ much from that in the Reference scenario, some applications and usage change because of investment, pricing, and service decisions by the Zaibatsu. For example, many more homes have direct fiber connections, but wireless devices and services are priced higher and thus used less than in the Reference scenario. More people live in smart homes with appliances, household inventories, and energy services managed automatically by a Zaibatsu subsidiary. Huge investments in intelligent transportation systems contribute to urban growth and the renewal of central city cores, but the resulting ease of commuting reduces the growth of telework from home. "Smart tagging" extends well beyond vehicles to include essentially all tangible goods above a nominal value. And nearly every public and (with permission or authorization) private space can be monitored on the Net.

3.4.2 ICT Issues in 2021

Although some Americans continue to object to the economic power and social controls the Zaibatsu and government exert, most accept them because of the security and stability they have brought to society. Proprietary hardware and software standards, along with well-enforced intellectual property rights to content, have partitioned the Net into eight well-functioning "walled gardens" with low-level paths of interoperability among them. But with self-healing software, government-licensed encryption and other centralized controls, and harsh penalties for infractions, the Net has never been more secure. Earlier concerns about a digital divide have vanished, since anyone who wants free access to the Net has it. Even privacy is less of a political issue than it was five years earlier: almost everyone recognizes that little privacy or anonymity exists in this Net-centered world and goes about his or her life accordingly. In 2021, as has been true for the preceding several years, the nation feels relatively secure and blessed with a robust economy buoyed by high acceptance and use of ICTs.

3.5 CYBERTOPIA SCENARIO

Cybertopia is a scenario in which the use and trust of networked ICTs is equally as high as that of the Zaibatsu scenario but where control of technology is much more distributed, falling predominately to in-

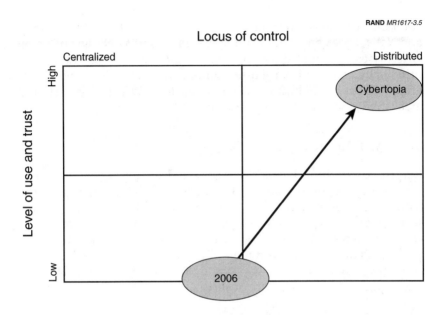

Figure 3.5—Cybertopia Scenario Progression from 2006

dividuals and to large and small organizations. Economic markets and consumer preferences largely determine the use of ICT products and services, with light government regulation and modest subsidies for low-income and other targeted groups.

The path toward Cybertopia assumes that after numerous hiccups in the first years of the new century, deregulation of communications, electricity, and other formerly regulated markets proceeds swiftly and successfully. Learning from early mistakes such as the Telecommunications Act of 1996, the Digital Millennium Copyright Act of 1998, the California electricity crisis of 2000–2001, and the draconian Antiterrorist Infrastructure Security Act of 2004, legislators, regulators, industry stakeholders, and consumers work together to create effective competitive markets for information, communications, and energy. Widespread adoption of open-source software and open, interoperable standards leads to renewed innovation and proliferation of affordable ICT devices and Net applications. ICT infrastructure investment is spurred by entrepreneurs and new partnerships among business, government, and nonprofit entities, in addition to established stakeholders. By 2021, the ICT infrastructure and Net services are owned and operated by a mix of large and small enterprises, many of them located close to the communities they principally serve. This structure supports and encourages more geographic dispersal of households and jobs to smaller towns and rural areas than is seen in the other scenarios.

3.5.1   ICT Applications and Usage

Robust competition keeps prices low and encourages ICT ownership and usage throughout the United States (Table 3.4). Compared with the Reference and Zaibatsu scenarios, Cybertopia emphasizes wireless over wired infrastructure, and greater use of consumer e-commerce, telework, distance learning, telemedicine, and embedded network sensors for environmental and process control. Nearly all residences have home networks, and 90 percent of households use energy management software or services linked to real-time prices.

3.5.2   ICT Issues in 2021

Although this scenario includes more networked devices and sensors than do the others, information technologies have been quite successful in helping individuals and organizations maintain levels of security and privacy they find acceptable. Net infrastructure and

Table 3.4

ICT Ownership and Use, Cybertopia Scenario

	Percentage	
	2006	2021
Adults with cell phone/PDA	70	95
Households with Net access	70	95
Households with broadband Net access	30	93
Households with multichannel TV	80	95
Households with fiber to the curb or home	<5	65
Households with digital TV receiver	8	98
Households with broadband home network	20	95
Households with networked EMS	10	90

service providers must guarantee basic privacy and security features, but users can choose (and pay for) upgraded firewalls and individualized software agents that give added levels of protection. In addition, the Personal Information Freedom and Responsibility Act of 2015 (PIFRA) has granted individuals legal ownership of their personal information, which they can choose to keep private, to trade in real-time markets, or to assign to software agents that know their requirements and preferences. Thus, for example, some people may give free use of their consumption data to trusted agents in order to receive advance notice of bargains and offers, others may demand payment for information about themselves, and still others may refuse to provide information at all. Complaints about privacy abuse have receded since the passage of PIFRA, in good part because of well-publicized cases in which individuals have been awarded substantial damages from commercial firms or government agencies that have misused their personal information.

Cybertopia has other ICT issues, however. Even with low prices, subsidies are sometimes needed to keep low-income households, the elderly, and those with disabilities connected to the Net. The Transparency Act of 2011, which mandated that (nearly) all government information be openly accessible on the Net, often brings conflicts with PIFRA and remains highly controversial 10 years after passage. Although software agents and filters are widely available, nearly everyone complains about information overload. And many voice concerns about continuing losses of programming, sales, and service intermediary jobs as autonomous agents take on more and more responsibility for commercial and consumer transactions. Still, most people like Cybertopia, even if it seems quite overwhelming at times.

3.6 NET INSECURITY SCENARIO

Compared to the other scenarios, Net Insecurity is much less optimistic: persistent, unresolved security problems reduce public trust in and usage of networked ICT applications and services. The path in this scenario begins with the vulnerabilities recognized in 2006, which soon worsen despite the best efforts of technologists, industry, and government to contain them. Neither technical security fixes nor harsh legal penalties are able to stop widespread penetration of the Net and the equipment connected to it by hackers, criminals, and

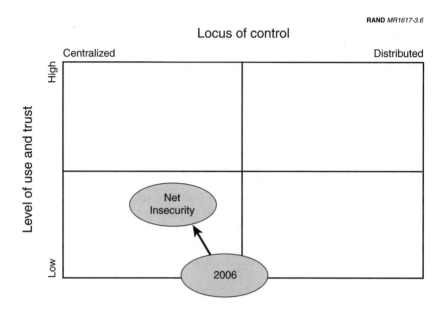

Figure 3.6—Net Insecurity Scenario Progression from 2006

other "information terrorists," many of whom are believed to operate from outside the United States. As a consequence, use of the public Net peaks around 2014 and then declines due to a series of unfortunate events:

- Identity theft and e-commerce losses rise to epidemic levels.

- Hackers repeatedly deface information sites and replace Netcam images with pornographic pictures.

- Over the winter of 2014–2015, several thousand patients whose heartbeats are being remotely monitored receive false signals that disable or destabilize their implanted pacemakers and defibrillators. Many are seriously injured, some die.

- Unknown malefactors penetrate "smart home" networks, remotely turning on ovens, ranges, and coffee pots while cutting off water supplies. Thousands of houses and apartments in hundreds of communities throughout the country burn down, causing much property damage, many injuries, and scores of deaths.

By 2016, most U.S. cities and states ban the connection of home networks to the public Net.

Such disasters spur the growth of private, highly secured, compartmentalized, and expensive networks that do not interconnect. Large businesses, government agencies, and others that can afford these private networks rely on them for information, communications, and transactions; everyone else must fend for him/herself on what has become a very insecure public Net.

3.6.1 ICT Applications and Usage

Consumers invest heavily in wireless communications, one-way media, and stand-alone ICT devices (Table 3.5). Cocooning at home with large-screen, high-definition video on disk or delivered by one-way satellite or cable/fiber network is very popular. Despite the public Net's insecurity, about 50 percent of households still connect using an isolated, voice-activated terminal principally to exchange video, voice, and text messages. Telework is rather limited; B2C e-commerce and home medical monitoring are virtually nonexistent. Information available on the public Net is not considered reliable, but many people enjoy the gossipy, often salacious material they can readily find. Home networks link devices within residences but remain islands unconnected to the public Net.

Table 3.5

ICT Ownership and Use, Net Insecurity Scenario

	Percentage	
	2006	2021
Adults with cell phone/PDA	70	90
Households with Net access	70	50
Households with broadband Net access	30	45
Households with cable or satellite TV	80	98
Households with fiber to the curb or home	<5	50
Households with digital TV receiver	8	99
Households with broadband home network	20	80
Households with networked EMS	10	70

Those who work for large or medium-sized organizations routinely use secure private networks at their offices. These networks have limited interoperability and several layers of authentication, which keep the volume of B2B e-commerce transactions well below those in the other scenarios. Distance learning is usually available at work, however.

3.6.2   ICT Issues in 2021

As of about 2014, a digital divide has existed between those who can use the relatively secure private networks, which are generally operated by large organizations, and everyone else. Secure private networks offer more opportunities for distance learning, telework, and e-commerce, as well as access to more-reliable information. The association of these advantages with large organizations has led to some recentralization of power and control, along with new calls for government action to bridge the gap between the information rich and information poor.

Even more troubling is the realization that 20 years of ICT investments have brought few real gains to most Americans. Unremitting battles with information terrorists have not only compromised the ICT infrastructure, but also damaged the electricity grid and many other important sectors of the U.S. economy. But there is little prospect of going back to a simpler life, one without information appliances and networks. The United States in 2021 seems truly like the Red Queen's world in *Through the Looking Glass*: everyone must keep running—i.e., spending enormous effort and wealth on ICT security—just to stay in the same place.

3.7   COMPARING THE SCENARIOS

While the evolutionary paths of the four scenarios differ considerably, their 2021 end points share a number of common features:

- ICT usage is well above the 2006 level, even in the dystopic Net Insecurity scenario;

- The vast majority of B2B transactions are done electronically;

- Voice, text, picture, and video traffic are well integrated on the ICT Nets that have replaced the separate telephone, cable, broadcast, and satellite networks of 2001;

- Most people hold conversations or send messages over wireless links, although the bits are likely to flow over fiber optic or other wired circuits for much of the distance;

- Specialized, mostly wireless devices have replaced PCs for most Net applications;

- Like electric motors in the 20th century, ICT technologies have become largely invisible as they have been embedded into devices and systems for ordinary use.

However, there are also significant differences among the four scenarios in 2021, as indicated in Table 3.6. These differences show up particularly in number of teleworkers, consumer use of e-commerce, and use of networked applications such as medical monitoring. The similarities and differences together reflect three themes in ICT development that have recurred over past decades and that we project into the 21st century: technology adoption takes place over decades, contradictory trends proceed simultaneously, and unplanned, mostly unintended consequences dominate the long-term effects of technology.

3.7.1 Technology Adoption Takes Place over Decades

Technology diffusion trends observable in 2001 are likely to still be in progress 20 years later. This is particularly true of technologies that require substantial infrastructure development, such as digital television and broadband Internet access. Even a relatively simple ICT device such as the telephone answering machine took more than 15 years to be adopted by 50 percent of U.S. telephone households after it was introduced in the early 1970s . Individuals and institutions change much more slowly than do ICTs, so rates of adoption and diffusion will determine how much impact a new development has by 2021.

Table 3.6

Comparisons of Scenarios

	2021 Scenario			
	Reference	Zaibatsu	Cybertopia	Net Insecurity
Adults with cell phone/PDA (%)	90	85	95	90
Households on Net (%)	92	98	95	50
Households with digital TV (%)	95	98	98	99
Households with fiber to the curb or home (%)	75	85	65	50
Large firms using e-commerce (%)	98	99	98	90
Consumers using e-commerce (%)	85	95	95	25
Medical monitoring on Net	Yes	More	More	Little
Teleworkers (million)	40	30	60	20
Devices connected to Net (billion)	4-6	5-10	>15	1
Open or proprietary software standards	Both	Prop.	Open	Prop.

3.7.2 Contradictory Trends Proceed Simultaneously

When a new ICT application presents itself, debates almost always arise as to whether it will substitute for or complement an older way of doing things. Usually it does both. For example, using the telephone or Internet sometimes substitutes for a face-to-face meeting, but it also sometimes encourages a meeting that might not otherwise occur. We believe that increased use of videoconferencing will have a similar, dual effect in the next two decades: it will substitute for some business and family travel and it will build personal relationships that inevitably lead to additional business and vacation trips.

3.7.3 Unplanned, Mostly Unintended Consequences Dominate the Long-Term Effects of Technology

As historians of technology have extensively documented, the telegraph, telephone, automobile, and television have changed settlement and work patterns, land usage, individual time budgets, and other aspects of lifestyle in ways that were neither planned nor anticipated. The same will almost certainly be true for the Internet and other ICTs in the future. In particular, ICT growth will have both unplanned and unexpected consequences for U.S. electricity requirements, which is the topic of the next chapter.

Chapter Four

IMPLICATIONS OF THE SCENARIOS FOR U.S. ELECTRICITY USE

In this chapter, we project the implications of the information and communications technology (ICT) scenarios for electricity consumption in the United States over the next 20 years and compare our results with the forecasts made by the U.S. Energy Information Administration (EIA) in the *AEO 2002* (Energy Information Administration, 2001). Our focus is on electricity use in the residential, commercial, and industrial sectors, because other sectors (notably, transportation) account for only a small percentage of current and projected electricity use.[1] Appendix B presents the assumptions we used in generating these projections.

4.1 HOW ICT INFLUENCES ELECTRICITY AND OTHER ENERGY USE

ICTs have three distinct influences on the use of electricity and other energy:

• Direct consumption of electricity by ICT equipment;

---

[1]We specifically do not include projections of net electricity consumption by electric or fuel-cell vehicles, primarily because we do not expect them to be significant purchasers or sellers of electricity in the United States by 2021. Some disagree with this assessment—see, for example, Hawken, Lovins, and Lovins, 1999. Consequently, we suggest in Chapter Six that subsequent research on ICT-driven electricity usage include prospective power purchases and sales by electric or fuel-cell vehicles.

- Changes in electricity use that are brought about by ICT-facilitated energy management systems (EMSs) in buildings;

- Changes in electricity and other energy usage that stem from business and societal changes associated with increased use of ICTs and the transition toward a digital society.

Electricity consumption by ICT equipment is the most direct and visible but not necessarily the most important of these three influences. Over time, the other two—energy management and broader socioeconomic trends—will likely have much more consequential effects on electricity and other energy use (Allenby and Unger, 2001). However, the fact that these two imply behavioral as well as technological changes makes them much more difficult to estimate. This is a principal reason for our developing several scenarios rather than a single projection. As one illustration, consider the enthusiasm for an ICT-driven "new economy" in the late 1990s that led some to forecast significant decreases in commercial floor space resulting from widespread adoption of e-commerce and telework, with large accompanying reductions in requirements for electricity and other forms of energy. Our Cybertopia scenario generally reflects this perspective, whereas the other three scenarios forecast smaller changes in shopping and commuting behaviors. Other factors, such as changing energy prices, demographics, and consumer preferences, will also strongly influence electricity use in a more digital society.

4.2 ELECTRICITY USE IN THE RESIDENTIAL SECTOR, 2001–2021

The *AEO 2002* projects that U.S. residential electricity consumption will increase from 1,230 billion kWh, or 1,230 terawatt-hours (TWh), in 2001 to 1,670 TWh in 2020—an average annual growth rate of 1.7 percent. More important for this analysis, the household electricity intensity—measured as the annual kilowatt-hours consumed per household (kWh/hh)—is projected to grow from 11,600 kWh/hh in 2001 to 13,200 kWh/hh in 2020 (Figure 4.1). This represents an average annual growth rate of 0.7 percent, which is well below the 4 percent average growth over the past 50 years as refrigerator/freezers, washers, dryers, televisions, and other electrical appliances became ubiquitous in American households.

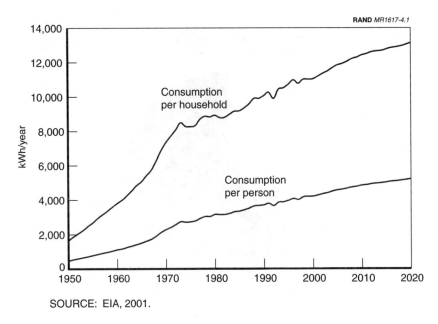

SOURCE: EIA, 2001.

Figure 4.1—Trends in Residential Electricity Use, 1950–2020

4.2.1   Residential Electricity Use by ICT Equipment

Electricity in the home is used mostly for space heating and cooling, water heating, lighting, and refrigeration. Recent studies at Lawrence Berkeley National Laboratory (LBNL) (Kawamoto et al., 2001; Rosen, Meier, and Zandelin, 2001; and Rosen and Meier, 1999 and 2000) estimate that ICT equipment accounted for only about 7 percent of total residential electricity use in 1999 (Figure 4.2), and that television and video equipment represented well over half of household ICT electricity use in 1999 (Figure 4.3).

Starting from the LBNL baseline data for 1999, we projected household ICT equipment inventories and electricity consumption for 2001 to 2021 for each of our scenarios.[2] Bottom-up estimates were developed for the four groups of ICT devices shown in Figure 4.3:

---

[2]Our projections through 2005 are generally consistent with those developed by Jon Peddie Associates for ICT devices in the home with "networking potential" (see Arrington, 2001).

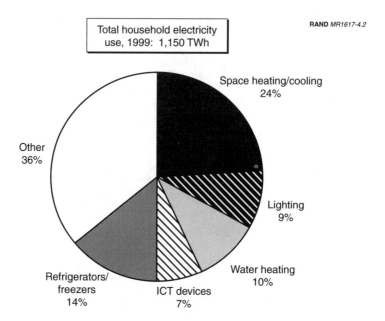

Figure 4.2—Electricity Use in the Residential Sector, 1999

1. *Computer and office equipment:* desktop, laptop, and notebook computers; personal digital assistants (PDAs); and printers, copiers, scanners, storage devices, and other computer peripherals or home office machinery.

2. *Television and video equipment:* both analog and digital television receivers; set-top boxes for receiving signals from terrestrial broadcast, satellite, cable, fiber optic, or other networks; VCRs, DVD players, video digital recorders, and other video devices; and game consoles.

3. *Audio equipment:* component, compact, and portable stereo systems; music recording and playing devices, such as current CD and MP3 players; and clock radios.

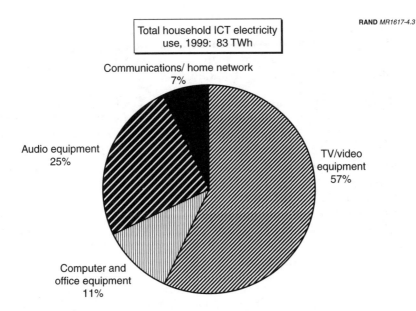

RAND *MR1617-4.3*

Total household ICT electricity
use, 1999: 83 TWh

Communications/ home network
7%

Audio equipment
25%

TV/video
equipment
57%

Computer and
office equipment
11%

SOURCES: Kawamoto et al., 2001; Rosen, Meier, and Zandelin, 2001;
Rosen and Meier, 1999 and 2000.

Figure 4.3—Electricity Use by Residential ICT Equipment, 1999

4. *Communications and home network equipment:* wired, cordless,
   and wireless phones; answering machines; fax machines (if not
   integrated with other home office equipment); home security systems; home networks connecting computer, office, and entertainment devices; and other home networks connecting appliances, lighting, and HVAC equipment.

We expect ICT devices that are separate in 2001 to undergo a good
deal of technical convergence and integration. For example, our scenarios assume that one-third of cell phones will have true PDA features by 2006, and that essentially all handheld (or smaller) wireless
devices will have integrated voice and data capabilities by 2015.

Similarly, today's analog audio and video equipment—stereo components and systems, television receivers, video recorders, and most set-top boxes—will become digital and largely integrated as households adopt digital television and replace their analog components.

At the same time, special-purpose ICT devices will proliferate in the home. Our Reference scenario posits that smart appliances will have more marketing pizzazz than actual use in the next five years, but that appliances purchased in 2006 or later will have embedded processors ready to be programmed and controlled over home networks and/or the Internet. Smart, networked devices for entertainment, communications, and information will substitute for general-purpose computers in many applications. Most households will still have at least one "old-fashioned" general-purpose computer in 2021, but they will also have dozens of specialized ICT devices for specific tasks and functions.

Future electricity use by ICT equipment in the home depends on a complex net balance between different, conflicting trends that favor higher (+) or lower (–) consumption. These trends include

+   Twenty-year growth in the U.S. population and in U.S. households of 18 and 21 percent, respectively;

+   Greater numbers of ICT devices at home in each of the four groups listed above;

–   Faster growth of wireless than of wired devices;[3]

+   Larger, more-powerful devices that consume more electricity in both active and standby mode, such as digital instead of analog television receivers;

–   More energy efficient chips and devices in all categories that cut active and standby power requirements;

+   Longer on-times for ICT equipment—e.g., computer and office equipment used by home workers and teleworkers, and comput-

---

[3]See, for example, Standage, 2001.

ers and other networked devices used for shopping, communicating, and playing games;[4]

– Use of ICT sensors and controls to manage electricity consumption more efficiently.

We took each of these trends into account in our projections of residential electricity use by ICT equipment. The projections are presented in Table 4.1 and discussed below (see Appendix B for further details).

4.2.1.1 Home computer and office equipment. Trends increasing electricity use include the continuation of Moore's Law: packing more components and functions into chips and devices,[5] near-ubiquitous penetration of more-powerful home computers with

Table 4.1

Residential Electricity Use by ICT Equipment, 2001–2021

			Electricity Use (TWh)			
				2021 Scenario		
	2001	2006	Reference	Zaibatsu	Cybertopia	Net Insecurity
Computer and home office equipment	14	19	25	29	30	22
TV and video equipment	47	55	88	89	88	117
Audio equipment	20	22	28	28	28	30
Communications and network equipment	8	14	52	56	58	43
Total ICT equipment	89	110	193	202	205	213

---

[4]Whether increased use of some devices will lead to decreased use of others remains an unanswered question. The UCLA Center for Communication Policy (2001) reports from its survey that Internet users in 2001 watched 4.5 fewer hours of television per week than did non-users. However, other studies, from the United States and Europe, did not find such differences. See, for example, Aebischer and Huser, 2000.

[5]Simple extrapolation of energy consumption in today's (2001) computer chips to that of much more powerful chips in five or ten years would lead to chip meltdown (see Corcoran, 2001). We assume in these scenarios that new chip designs, new materials, and better cooling methods will allow continued exploitation of Moore's Law for the next two decades.

larger displays, always-on broadband connections to the Net, broad-band home networks, more home offices, and (except in the Net In-security scenario) teleworking. These are balanced to a great extent by the more-energy-efficient design of chips and equipment with built-in power management, universal adoption of flat-panel dis-plays using less than half the power per square inch of CRT displays (Norford et al., 1990; and Groot and Siderius, 2000),[6] and a general trend away from high-power desktop computers and toward wireless laptop and handheld devices.

Without these mitigating trends, electricity use by home computer and office equipment in 2021 would be more than 50 percent higher than the figures shown in Table 4.1. With them, electricity use by home computer and office equipment in the Reference scenario grows from 14 TWh in 2001 to 25 TWh in 2021—an average annual growth rate of 3.1 percent. Our estimates are somewhat below the *AEO 2002* EIA (2001) estimates, which project that electricity use by residential computers will increase from 15 TWh in 2001 to 34 TWh in 2021, for an average annual increase of 4.2 percent. Compared with those projections, ours assume more rapid growth in the num-ber of home computers over the 20 years, but less average power consumption per unit as wireless devices capture a larger share of the home market.

Even in the high-ICT-use scenarios of Cybertopia and Zaibatsu, power consumption in 2021 by home computer and office equip-ment amounts to less than 15 percent of the total power needed for residential ICT equipment, and less than 2 percent of total residential electricity consumption. On the basis of kilowatt-hours demanded, the greatly expanded role that both we and EIA project for computers and other information appliances in the home will not heavily bur-den U.S. electricity supplies. However, the need for higher power quality and reliability (PQR) for these digital devices does represent an important issue, one that we consider in Chapter Five.

4.2.1.2 Television, video, and audio equipment. Electricity con-sumption by television and video equipment grows more rapidly

---

[6]Displays based on organic light-emitting devices (OLEDs) that are in development at IBM and elsewhere would consume less energy per square inch than do current flat-panel liquid crystal displays (LCDs).

after 2006 in all four of our scenarios as digital television equipment becomes cheaper and its household penetration increases. The 2001–2021 average annual growth rate in the Reference scenario is 3.2 percent, which is very close to that in the *AEO 2002* projections. The benefits from conversion to flat-panel displays and from general energy efficiency improvements are outweighed by consumers' desire for more-integrated video equipment with larger screens in more rooms. Electricity consumption in 2021 is 34 percent greater in the Net Insecurity than in the Reference scenario, because consumers choose even more-elaborate digital video systems rather than investing in equipment connected to an insecure Net. We project similar but less important differences among the scenarios for electricity use by home audio equipment.

4.2.1.3 Home communications and network equipment. At present, electricity consumption by communications and network equipment in the home (primarily telephones, answering machines, fax machines, and security systems) accounts for less than 9 percent of the total power consumed by all ICT equipment. We project that the 9 percent will grow to more than 25 percent by 2021 in the Reference, Zaibatsu, and Cybertopia scenarios, when nearly all residences will have always-on broadband networks using a combination of wired and wireless links. Home networks generally will first be used to interconnect computer, home office, and entertainment equipment; but by 2021, most will also control the home environment (heating, ventilation, air conditioning, and lighting) and many appliances. The result will be large increases in electricity consumed to power not only 120 million home networks, but also the 20 to 25 billion wired or wireless sensors, actuators, controllers, and human interfaces that these applications will demand.

4.2.2 Electricity Savings from ICT-Facilitated Energy Management in Residences

While adding to electricity consumption, a home network can also contribute to electricity savings as part of a home energy management system (EMS) that includes such features as programmable control of heating, cooling and lighting systems, remote control via the Internet, and responsiveness to weather conditions, household routines and electricity prices (Lewis, 2000). Following a recent paper by Rabaey et al. (2001), we outline here the three phases in home network EMS development that we used to estimate reductions in residential electricity consumption in the scenarios.

In phase 1, which largely entails passive monitoring, the EMS gathers data from various sensors about local conditions (temperature, lighting, equipment usage), displays the data, and implements control decisions made by the end user. These decisions may be made manually on a case-by-case basis (e.g., turn on the air conditioning in the master bedroom) or automatically using simple devices such as timers or thermostats. The growing availability of cheap (wired or wireless) sensors linked together on the home network allows such monitoring and control at the level of individual rooms or appliances.

The phase 2 EMS goes beyond passive monitoring, providing current data about energy consumption and prices and computing current and/or projected costs to the household. This encourages users to make cost-saving decisions when prices are high. This phase requires installation of digital electricity meters in the home that are linked to the home EMS, implementation of time-of-use (TOU) or real-time pricing (RTP),[7] and provision of the means to make price data routinely available to the home EMS (e.g., over the Internet).

The phase 3 EMS actively manages energy use, gathering local and external data and applying the household's programmed rules and preferences (e.g., keep bedroom temperatures between 65 and 72 degrees when occupied, but turn down the air conditioning if the electricity price goes above 15 cents/kWh). Phase 3 embodies the "smart home" concept that has been demonstrated and widely publicized but not yet widely deployed. The technical path seems clear, however: home EMSs will use distributed sensors, actuators, and other microprocessor-based devices to manage the home environment and appliances under the supervision of a central control unit.

---

[7]Time-of-use pricing refers to electricity pricing that varies predictably by time of day (e.g., a high peak-load rate between 8am and 6pm on weekdays, and a lower off-peak rate at other times). Real-time prices are set more frequently (usually hourly) to reflect the underlying wholesale price of power, and can rise steeply when demand peaks or supply is curtailed. See Reed, 2001.

Over time, home EMSs will evolve to become considerably more capable, complex, and autonomous.

Estimates of the energy savings from phase 1, 2, and 3 home EMSs vary greatly and are supported by few empirical data from the residential sector. A few pilot projects with residential TOU electricity pricing have been conducted (e.g., Aubin et al., 1995), and a larger program involving some 300,000 customers is now under way in the state of Washington (Brock, 2001). RTP, which economists expect to match electricity supply and demand more efficiently than TOU does, has primarily been implemented in voluntary programs for large industrial and commercial customers. Data from such programs at Georgia Power, Duke Power, and GPU Energy show peak load reductions of 10 to 50 percent, with consistently larger responses at higher prices (EPRI, 2001). At the residential level, the Edison Electric Institute estimated in the mid-1990s that RTP could reduce overall electricity consumption by as much as 5 percent (National Institute of Standards and Technology, 1994). This upper bound is consistent with one RTP "natural experiment" among residential customers in San Diego, California, who reduced electricity consumption by an average of 5.2 percent during August 1999 when their rates more than doubled (EPRI, 2001).

However, except for situations in which electricity prices become very high such as was the case in San Diego, there is scant evidence that residential customers will actually use RTP when it is available. Consumers are generally risk averse and favor simple, predictable prices for utility-like services; e.g., they favor flat-rate over measured-use telephone service, and fixed monthly charges over pay-per-view for premium movie channels on satellite or cable TV. As one energy consultant reports: "[w]hen we listen to customers discuss what they need and what is important to them, we find RTP is seldom a good fit. In fact, most customers are willing to pay a premium over RTP for more simplicity and certainty in their pricing" (EnerVision, 1998). This suggests that there is an intermediary role for distribution utilities or other energy service companies that buy power at variable rates and repackage it to sell to consumers at (presumably higher) fixed rates, in addition to selling other home energy management services. In Zaibatsu, the vertically integrated utilities provide such services, whereas in Cybertopia, many large and small firms compete to offer them to residential customers.

Most studies of phase 3 EMS focus on commercial buildings, where the prospective economic returns are more clear-cut than they are for residences. At the high end, Raebey et al. (2001, p. 3) estimate that smart commercial buildings could reduce "lighting power consumption by 40%" and "energy dissipation for space conditioning . . . by 44%." Romm (1999, p. 18) cites estimates of potential 25 percent savings in energy consumption from installing digital EMSs in 24 commercial buildings in Texas. However, EPRI's Consortium for Electric Infrastructure to Support a Digital Society (2001a, p. 20) projects only "up to 2.5%" savings from EMSs in commercial buildings. Kris Pister, leader of a University of California at Berkeley research project on tiny wireless sensors for energy monitoring and management, estimates that using this "smart dust" on the Berkeley campus could cut "power use by at least 5 percent" (Ainsworth, 2001).

For our scenarios, we estimate reductions in electricity consumption for space conditioning and lighting of 3, 9, and 15 percent for households that adopt phase 1, 2, and 3 EMSs, respectively. We assume the distribution of phase 1, 2, and 3 EMS households is as shown in Table 4.2, which leads to the power savings also shown there. Only in Cybertopia do the electricity savings from EMSs exceed the power consumed by home networks. This finding reflects our view that households install home networks primarily to connect computer and office equipment and entertainment devices, with energy management usually following as an ancillary objective. But besides lowering overall electricity use, home EMSs linked to real-time prices reduce peak electricity demand and cut consumption of gas and other residential fuels. These savings have more important implications for energy and economic efficiency than do the changes in total kilowatt-hours consumed.

4.2.3   Changes in Residential Electricity Use from Telework

Cheaper, faster, and better ICTs enable more people to work from home on at least a part-time basis.[8] Based on the Telework America Survey 2000, which was conducted in the summer of 2000, the Inter-

---

[8]For an introduction to the substantial body of literature that has arisen on teleworking over the past two decades, see Nilles, 1998.

Table 4.2

Electricity Savings from Home Energy Management, 2001–2021

| | | | 2021 Scenario | | | |
| | | | | | | Net |
	2001	2006	Reference	Zaibatsu	Cybertopia	Insecurity
Households with EMS (%)						
Phase 1 (3% savings)	2	7	20	20	10	40
Phase 2 (9% savings)	0	2	20	25	20	20
Phase 3 (15% savings)	0	1	30	35	60	10
Total	2	10	70	80	90	70
Electricity savings (TWh)	–0.3	–2.5	–39	–45	–62	–25
Home network power use (TWh)	7.9	14	52	56	58	43

national Telework Association and Council estimates that some 16.5 million regularly employed U.S. adults, about 9 percent of the adult work force, used ICT to work outside their offices at least one day per month (Nilles, 2000). More than 90 percent teleworked from home, using a combination of telephone, fax, computer, and the Internet. Fewer than 20 percent were full-time teleworkers.

The first-order effect of telework is greater electricity consumption at home. Both the Telework America Survey 2000 and a recent study of telework in Switzerland by Aebischer and Huser (2000) found that teleworking households have an average of one computer more than non-telework households. Not surprisingly, they also found that teleworkers use computers as well as home printers, scanners, and other ICT devices much more intensively than do non-teleworkers. Based on these studies and our projections for teleworking through 2021, we arrived at estimates, shown in Table 4.3, of the incremental home electricity use for teleworking for each of the four scenarios.[9] Space conditioning and lighting, both directly in the home office and indirectly in the rest of the house, consume more power than does

---

[9]Power consumption estimates in all categories are incremental to those projected without teleworking. Power for space conditioning also assumes that the size of the average house increases by 6 percent between 2001 and 2021, an estimate taken from EIA, 2001.

Table 4.3

Annual Incremental Home Electricity Use for Telework, 2001–2021

			2021 Scenario			
	2001	2006	Reference	Zaibatsu	Cybertopia	Net Insecurity
Teleworkers (million)	17	25	40	30	60	20
% of adult work force	9	13	18	13	28	9
avg. telework days/week	2.0	2.1	2.5	2.0	3.0	2.0
Electricity use (TWh)						
Home office						
ICT equipment	3.0	4.4	7.2	4.3	13	2.9
Lighting	2.0	2.9	4.4	2.6	7.9	1.8
Space conditioning	6.8	11	20	12	36	8
Home office–subtotal	12	18	32	19	57	13
Rest of house	8	12	21	13	38	8
Total	20	30	53	32	95	21

the teleworker's ICT equipment. Sixty percent of the total incremental electricity is used in the home office, with the remaining 40 percent used for space conditioning, hot water, lighting, and appliances in the rest of the house (Aebischer and Huser, 2000, p. 40).

In 2001, our average teleworker's home office used an additional 870 kWh, compared with the 750 kWh estimated by Romm (1999). Total incremental consumption in the teleworker's home is 1,450 kWh, compared with an estimate of 1,650 kWh cited by Aebischer and Huser (2000).

While teleworking increases electricity use at home, it also permits employers to cut back on floor space and ICT equipment at their offices. These effects are discussed in Sections 4.3 and 4.4, which cover commercial and industrial electricity consumption. The net impact on electricity consumption depends on the division of time between work at the office and work at home. A once-a-week teleworker usually has a home office and exclusive use of an office that he/she commutes to, and the electricity consumption for the two offices in this case will generally exceed that for a one-office, full-time commuter. A four-day-a-week teleworker, however, most often shares an office away from home with other workers, producing lower net electricity consumption.[10] And teleworkers use less fuel commuting to and from work, although they make more local trips on days they telecommute from home.[11]

4.2.4 Summing Up: ICT-Driven Residential Electricity Use, 2001–2021

The combined effects on residential power consumption for ICT equipment, EMSs, and telework, which constitute our "ICT-driven subtotal," are shown in Table 4.4 and Figure 4.4. To use 2001 as a baseline for comparing our projections with those in the *AEO 2002*, we assume that our results for audio equipment and home communications/network equipment are included in the *AEO 2002* estimates for "other uses," and that our results for EMSs and telework in 2001 are included in the *AEO 2002* estimates for space heating, space cooling, and lighting. This makes our 2001 total match that in the *AEO 2002*, although the components differ: our ICT-driven subtotal is larger than the one in the *AEO 2002*, and our non-ICT subtotal is smaller. For consistency with the *AEO 2002* projections beyond 2001, our non-ICT subtotal in future years increases at the same rate as the non-ICT subtotal in the *AEO 2002*.

The effect of increased business-to-consumer (B2C) e-commerce on residential electricity use is largely captured in the ICT equipment category. We expect other e-commerce effects on residential power consumption to be quite limited, although B2C e-commerce will affect vehicle miles traveled (VMT) and thus fuel consumption by consumer and delivery vehicles. We have made separate projections for e-commerce effects on commercial and industrial electricity use (see Sections 4.3 and 4.4).

---

[10]Aebischer and Huser (2000, p. 41) discuss a 2000 study of telework in a Swiss bank that was conducted by Schmeider et al. That study assumes that four teleworkers save three office work desks and estimates that the net change in annual electricity use is +115 kWh for a one-day-a-week teleworker and –282 kWh for a four-day-a-week teleworker.

[11]Mokhtarian (1998) estimates that a day spent teleworking from home reduces the worker's vehicle miles traveled on that day by at most 60 percent.

Table 4.4

ICT Effects on Residential Electricity Use, 2001–2021

| | | | Electricity Use (TWh) | | | |
| | | | | 2021 Scenario | | |
	2001	2006	Reference	Zaibatsu	Cybertopia	Net Insecurity
ICT equipment	89	110	193	202	205	213
EMSs	0	–3	–39	–45	–62	–25
Telework	20	30	53	32	95	21
Subtotal ICT-driven	108	137	207	188	237	208
Subtotal non-ICT[a]	1,120	1,240	1,520	1,520	1,520	1,520
Total residential[a]	1,230	1,380	1,720	1,700	1,750	1,720
EIA total residential[a]	1,230	1,370	1,700	1,700	1,700	1,700
Difference from EIA	0	8	23	4	53	24
Difference from EIA as a %	0	0.6	1.3	0.2	3.1	1.4

[a]Rounded to three significant figures.

For the Reference scenario, the ICT-driven subtotal in Table 4.4 nearly doubles between 2001 and 2021, representing an average annual growth rate of 3.3 percent. The percentage of residential electricity consumption that is ICT-driven rises from 9 percent in 2001 to 11 percent in 2021, due principally to increased power consumption from digital video equipment, home networks, and telework-related office equipment. The total residential consumption projected for the Reference scenario for 2021 is 23 TWh, or 1.3 percent, above that projected in the *AEO 2002*.[12]

With more telework than the other scenarios have, Cybertopia shows the highest residential power consumption: 237 TWh, representing 13.5 percent of the total for the residential sector. The totals for Zaibatsu and Net Insecurity fall between those for the Reference and Cybertopia scenarios. However, even Cybertopia's total is only 53 TWh, or 3.1 percent, higher than that projected in the *AEO 2002*. And as discussed in the next two sections, the increases are more than

---

[12]We used the *AEO 2002* average annual growth rate of 1.7 percent to extend the *AEO 2002* projected total for residential electricity consumption from 1,672 TWh in 2020 to 1,700 TWh in 2021.

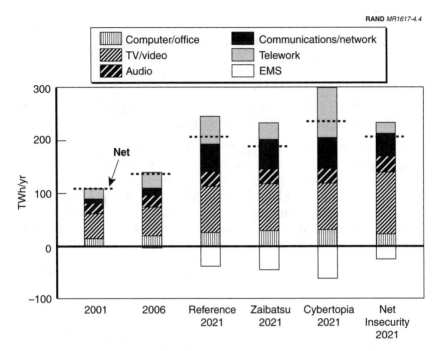

NOTE: Electricity savings (e.g., from EMSs) are shown as negative TWh/yr. The "net" lines show the sum of the negative and positive components for each year and scenario.

Figure 4.4—ICT-Driven Residential Electricity Use, 2001–2021

offset by decreases in electricity consumption in the commercial and industrial sectors from ICT-driven energy management, e-commerce, and telework.

4.3   ELECTRICITY USE IN THE COMMERCIAL SECTOR, 2001–2021

The commercial sector comprises all activities other than those classified as residential, industrial, or transportation. It includes education, health care, lodging, telecommunications, professional services, wholesale and retail trade, government services, religious groups, and other private, nonprofit, and public organizations.

The vast majority of energy use in the commercial sector occurs in buildings, both to maintain the building environment and to provide building-based services. The *AEO 2002* projects that electricity intensity in the commercial sector—defined as kilowatt-hours consumed annually per square foot of commercial floor space—will increase from 17.7 kWh/ft^2 in 2001 to 20.1 kWh/ft^2 in 2020, an average annual increase of 0.6 percent (Figure 4.5).

ICT can influence commercial electricity use in two principal ways: by changing the electricity intensity in commercial buildings and by changing the amount of floor space required for commercial activities. The power demands of ICT equipment and the electricity savings from EMSs in commercial buildings affect electricity intensity; such ICT-driven changes as e-commerce and telework primarily affect floor space requirements.

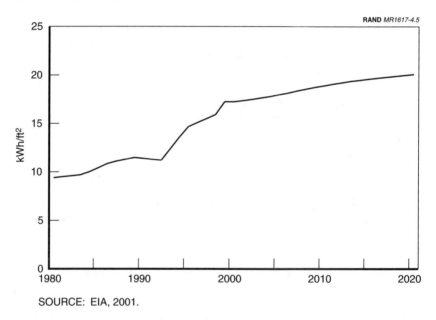

SOURCE: EIA, 2001.

Figure 4.5—Electricity Intensity Trends in Commercial Buildings, 1980–2020

4.3.1   Commercial Electricity Use by ICT Equipment

Baseline 1999–2000 estimates of electricity consumption by ICT equipment in the commercial sector can be found in the *AEO 2002* (EIA, 2001), LBNL studies by Kawamoto et al. (2001) and Koomey et al. (1999), and a study by Roth, Goldstein, and Kleinman (2000) published by Arthur D. Little, Inc. (ADL). These estimates differ substantially (see Table 4.5) because of different years of estimation,[13] different sector definitions,[14] and several other factors.[15]

To develop a baseline estimate for our scenario projections, we started with the ADL figures for 2000 (shown in Table 4.5), since they represent the most recent and most disaggregated, bottom-up esti-

Table 4.5

Estimates of Electricity Use by Commercial ICT Equipment, 1999–2000

	Estimated Electricity Use (TWh)		
	EIA	LBNL	ADL
Office computer equipment[a]	47	29	48
Other office equipment	94	24	37
Network equipment[b]	n/a[c]	15	13
Total ICT equipment	141	68	97

[a]Includes portable and desktop computers, terminals, monitors, and printers.

[b]Includes both computer network and telecommunications network equipment.

[c]Not applicable.

SOURCES: EIA, 2001; Kawamoto et al., 2001; Koomey et al., 1999; Roth, Goldstein, and Kleinman, 2002.

---

[13]The EIA and ADL figures are for 2000. The LBNL estimates are for 1999, except in the case of the Koomey et al. estimate of electricity used by telephone central offices, which is for 1997.

[14]The EIA and LBNL estimates are for the commercial sector, whereas the ADL estimate is for both the commercial and the industrial sector.

[15]These include different assumptions about standby and active use, different definitions of "other" office equipment, and different methods of estimation (Alan Meier, LBNL, personal communication, 2001).

mates. We adjusted these data to cover the commercial sector only, using the ratios of commercial/industrial electricity use by ICT equipment developed in the LBNL study by Kawamoto et al. (2001). We then extrapolated the results to 2001 using the 2000–2001 growth rates in the *AEO 2002* for electricity consumption by commercial sector ICT equipment.

These calculations yield a baseline estimate for our 2001 Reference scenario of 92 TWh for electricity consumption by ICT equipment in the commercial sector, which constitutes less than 8 percent of the 1,170 TWh estimated in the *AEO 2002* for total sector consumption in 2001 (Figure 4.6). The estimates in the *AEO 2002* show ICT equipment accounting for 152 TWh, or 13 percent, of commercial sector consumption in 2001; but we believe this figure is much too high in light of the recent LBNL and ADL data.

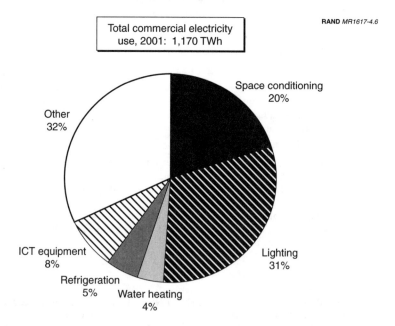

SOURCES: RAND calculation for ICT equipment; EIA, 2001, for other estimates.

Figure 4.6—Electricity Use in the Commercial Sector, 2001

The electricity use projections through 2021 in our scenarios fall well below those in the *AEO 2002* (Table 4.6). While much of the difference results from our lower baseline in 2001, we also project lower growth in power consumption by office ICT equipment over time than does EIA, principally because we assume that greater efficiency improvements and more telework will result in lower numbers of office computers and related ICT equipment.

We project growing electricity consumption in Internet data centers and by computer and telecommunications network equipment, which the EIA projections do not capture. The rapid growth of "Web server farms," "Internet hotels," and other data centers during the Internet boom of the late 1990s was thought likely to stress electricity distribution systems in places such as Silicon Valley, New York City, and Austin, Texas. These facilities have very high power densities, run continuously, and require more reliable power than do other electricity users.[16] As shown in Table 4.6, electricity consumption by

Table 4.6

Projected Electricity Use by ICT Equipment in Commercial Sector, 2001–2021

	Electricity Use (TWh)					
			2021 Scenario			
	2001	2006	Reference	Zaibatsu	Cybertopia	Net Insecurity
Office computer equipment	45	50	65	70	50	90
Other office equipment	29	35	45	50	40	70
Data centers	4	10	26	30	20	18
Network equipment	14	20	42	46	38	41
Total ICT equipment	92	115	178	196	148	219
EIA total ICT equipment	152	204	346	346	346	346
Difference from EIA as a %	−39	−44	−49	−43	−57	−37

---

[16]Data center power requirements are detailed in Mitchell-Jackson et al., 2001; and Mitchell-Jackson, 2001. The latter quotes estimates of data center square footage growth from 1998 to 2000 by Yankee Group (2000) (available at www.yankeegroup.com). Also see Park, 2000; and Templin, 2001.

data centers in 2001 is estimated at about 4 TWh, or about one-third of 1 percent of total sector use.

Simply extrapolating the 1998–2000 growth of data centers forward in time, however, would have them using more power than all the rest of the commercial sector well before 2010. This will not happen, of course. Data center expansion has slowed considerably since the dot.com bubble burst in 2000. The largest Web server farm company declared bankruptcy in 2001, and many Internet hotels remain vacant.

From a technical perspective, low-power computer chips will improve the energy efficiency of ICT equipment in data centers (IBM, 2001), but higher-performance equipment will require greater power density. The net effect in our projections for data centers is a modest increase in power density and restrained growth in square footage. Overall, we project that power used by data centers, along with commercial use of the Net in general, will continue to grow over the next 20 years. We estimate that by 2021, data centers will account for between 1 percent of commercial sector electricity consumption (Net Insecurity scenario) and 1.7 percent (Zaibatsu scenario).

Network equipment consists of the routers, switches, and hubs used in local area networks (LANs) and wide area networks (WANs), as well as the switches and other ICT equipment found in telephone central offices, PBXs, fiber optic transmission facilities, cellular base stations, and cable headends.[17] We anticipate considerable technological convergence among these categories over the next 20 years, as well as movement of network equipment from dedicated telephone and cable facilities into the more general-purpose data centers discussed above.

Countervailing power consumption trends again include greater energy efficiency at the component and device levels, offset by higher capacity, performance, and reliability requirements that demand more power. For example, each new generation of fiber optic terminals is much more energy efficient than the last on a watt-per-bit

---

[17]Roth, Goldstein, and Kleinman (2002, pp. 66–96) provide detailed estimates of electricity consumption in 2000 by these components of computer networks and telecommunications networks.

basis, but a fiber optic transmission facility still draws more power than the wire or cable facility it replaces. This becomes important in our scenarios as digital, always-on fiber-to-the-curb or fiber-to-the-home begins to penetrate the residential market after 2006.

As shown in Table 4.6, the differences between our projections and those in the *AEO 2002* for electricity consumption by commercial sector ICT equipment increase over time as a result of the various factors discussed above. Starting from a 2001 baseline estimate that is 60 TWh (39 percent) below that of the *AEO 2002*, the difference by 2021 is –168 TWh (–49 percent) for the Reference scenario and from –127 TWh (–37 percent) to –198 TWh (–57 percent) for the other three scenarios.

4.3.2 Electricity Savings from ICT-Facilitated Energy Management in Commercial Buildings

Building EMSs will become more generally adopted over the next 20 years and will use much more sophisticated ICT. Our projections for electricity savings in commercial buildings use the three EMS phases previously described for the residential sector:

- Phase 1: largely passive monitoring;

- Phase 2: real-time pricing;

- Phase 3: active, "intelligent" monitoring and management.

The electricity savings from each phase are assumed to be higher in the commercial than in the residential sector for several reasons. First, EMS savings come principally from space conditioning and lighting, which account for more than one-half of electricity consumption in the commercial sector, versus one-third in the residential sector. Commercial buildings generally use more power per square foot than do residences. Second, commercial building owners and/or tenants have clear bottom-line interests in managing their electricity use when the savings justify the EMS investment. Stated differently, commercial firms generally are more willing than households to pay up-front costs that will generate positive returns over the longer run. The commercial sector also offers better prospects for energy service companies or other intermediaries who may assume some of the initial EMS costs in return for downstream payments. Finally, using better sensors, faster microprocessors, and Internet-based monitoring reduces EMS costs while increasing performance, thus making EMS cost effective for niche commercial building applications.[18]

For commercial buildings with phase 1, 2, and 3 EMS, we estimate 6, 16, and 24 percent reductions, respectively, in electricity consumption for space conditioning and lighting. If we then assume the distribution of EMS phase 1, 2, and 3 buildings shown in Table 4.7, electricity savings for the Reference scenario increase from 2.6 TWh in 2001 to 76.4 TWh in 2021. Cybertopia, with abundant Net services and efficient markets for electricity management, has 36 percent greater electricity savings than does the Reference scenario. Even Net Insecurity exhibits a respectable 64 TWh in savings, although its commercial buildings must use more-costly private networks for EMS.

Table 4.7

Electricity Savings from Commercial Building Energy Management, 2001–2021

			2021 Scenario			
	2001	2006	Reference	Zaibatsu	Cybertopia	Net Insecurity
Buildings with EMS (%)						
Phase 1 (6% savings)	10	20	20	20	15	20
Phase 2 (16% savings)	0	15	25	25	25	20
Phase 3 (24% savings)	0	5	30	35	50	25
Total EMS buildings (%)	10	40	75	80	90	65
Electricity savings (TWh)	–3.6	–31	–91	–100	–120	–77

---

[18]For example, a hotel can set up its EMS so that the front-desk clerk turns on the space conditioning unit in an individual room when a guest checks in, and sensors subsequently readjust the temperature whenever the room is vacant for more than 15 minutes. A residential analogue might be the use of a cell phone to turn on air conditioning in one room five minutes before arriving home, but we do not expect this to be an important home application.

4.3.3   Changes in Commercial Electricity Use from E-Commerce

E-commerce has the potential to lower commercial sector electricity consumption, primarily by reducing the amount of commercial floor space required for Internet sales vis-à-vis in-store sales. According to the most recent Commercial Buildings Energy Consumption Survey (CBECS) (1995), retail establishments represent 15.5 percent of commercial floor space and 13.7 percent of commercial electricity consumption. Online sellers of books, music, computer hardware and software, and other items do not need large, well-lit, fully stocked retail stores to draw customers. Instead, their operations require data centers, upstream warehouses, and fulfillment and delivery services.

Comparing the floor space needs of these two very different ways of doing business is tricky, particularly since e-commerce operations are still evolving rapidly.[19] Although some early estimates claim floor space reductions of 80 to 90 percent for B2C online sales,[20] these seem overstated when total enterprise space needs, rather than the marginal space required to sell an additional unit, are considered.[21] Consequently, our scenarios estimate that an average of 50 percent less commercial floor space is needed for B2C e-commerce sales, which in the Reference scenario are projected to grow from 2 percent of retail sales in 2001[22] to 20 percent in 2021 (Table 4.8). The resulting reduction in electricity consumption is 15.6 TWh, or close to 1 percent of the total projected for the commercial sector in 2021. The

---

[19]As an illustration, Amazon.com, the leading online bookstore, has invested heavily in its own warehouses. Other B2C sellers rely more on drop-shipping from distributors or manufacturers.

[20]For example, based on a 1998 case study of Amazon.com by the Kellogg Graduate School of Management at Northwestern University, Romm, Rosenfeld, and Herrmann (1999, p. 26) state that *"a plausible estimate for the ratio of commercial building energy consumption per book sold for traditional stores versus online stores is 16 to 1"* (emphasis in original).

[21]The trend toward enterprises selling both online and through traditional stores also acts to moderate the floor space differences between channels, especially if and as e-commerce grows to become a substantial fraction of total sales.

[22]The 2 percent estimate is based on surveys conducted through November 2001 (see Forrester Research, 2002). Forrester's and several other projections of e-commerce revenues through 2005 are available at eMarketer, http://www. emarketer.com.

Table 4.8

Changes in Commercial Electricity Use from E-Commerce, 2001–2021

	2001	2006	2021 Scenario			
			Reference	Zaibatsu	Cybertopia	Net Insecurity
Business-to-consumer (B2C)						
Sales online (%)	2	7	20	25	35	7
Retail floor space saved with online sales (%)	50	50	50	50	50	50
Change in electricity consumption (TWh)	−1.5	−5.5	−15.6	−19.5	−27.3	−5.5
Business-to-business (B2B)						
Sales online (%)	5	20	70	75	80	60
Warehouse space saved with online sales (%)	10	10	10	10	10	10
Change in electricity consumption (TWh)	−0.4	−1.5	−5.4	−5.8	−6.2	−4.6
Change in electricity consumption: B2C+B2B (TWh)	−1.9	−7.0	−21	−25	−34	−10

projected reductions are 25 percent higher in Zaibatsu (19.5 TWh) and 50 percent higher in Cybertopia (27.3 TWh), but 65 percent lower in Net Insecurity (5.5 TWh), where consumers have lost confidence in B2C e-commerce.

B2B e-commerce can reduce inventories throughout the commercial and industrial sectors by streamlining distribution, shortening sales cycles, and improving marketing models. Lower inventories affect the industrial sector the most (see Subsection 4.4.3), but they also result in the need for less warehouse space in the commercial sector. Warehouses represent 14.4 percent of commercial floor space and 6.8 percent of commercial electricity consumption (Commercial Buildings Energy Consumption Survey, 1995). Our scenarios assume that B2B e-commerce sales reduce warehouse floor space requirements by 10 percent.[23] The resulting reduction in commercial sector power consumption in 2021 is between 4.6 TWh (Net Insecurity) and 6.2 TWh (Cybertopia). Here, the narrow range of impacts results from the relatively high penetration of B2B e-commerce by 2021 in all scenarios—even in Net Insecurity, where businesses still find economic benefits in using high-cost private networks to make B2B transactions.

4.3.4   Changes in Commercial Sector Electricity Use from Telework

As discussed in Subsection 4.2.3, telework increases residential electricity consumption and, because it reduces the need for office floor space, lowers commercial and industrial electricity consumption. Teleworkers still require office space, however, since most telework is part-time. We assumed a 20 percent reduction in office floor space and associated electricity consumption for each day per week spent teleworking—i.e., a 20 percent reduction for a one-day-per-week teleworker and an 80 percent reduction for a four-day-per-week teleworker. This estimate falls between other estimates of reduced office space for teleworkers.[24] We also used the CBECS (1995) figure of 387 ft^2 for average office size. Based on CBECS and EIA data (EIA, 2001, Table 5) on past and projected office electricity consumption, we project that annual electricity use per square foot of office space will increase from 19.6 kWh in 2001 to 22.3 kWh in 2020. Finally, applying the projections of numbers of teleworkers from our scenarios and assuming that 75 percent of teleworkers are in the commercial sector,[25] we arrive at the changes in commercial sector electricity consumption shown in Table 4.9.

---

[23]Romm (1999, p. 33) estimates that B2B e-commerce will yield a net reduction in warehouse floor space of 1 billion square feet, or about 12 percent, by 2007.

[24]JALA International, Inc. (1998), a consulting firm specializing in telework, estimates that a 1.5-day-per-week teleworker saves 150 ft^2, or 38 percent of the 387 ft^2 average office. Aebischer and Huser (2000, p. 41) estimate 75 percent office space savings for a four-day-per-week teleworker.

[25]Workers can telework more easily in some job categories (e.g., computer programmers) than in others (e.g., food service employees). Our review of Bureau of Labor Statistics data and projections on job categories (Bureau of Labor Statistics, 1999) led us to conclude that roughly 30 percent of workers in both the commercial and the industrial sector have high or moderately high potential for teleworking. The 75

Table 4.9

Changes in Commercial Electricity Use from Telework, 2001–2021

			2021 Scenario			
	2001	2006	Reference	Zaibatsu	Cybertopia	Net Insecurity
Teleworkers in sector (million)	12.8	18.8	30	22.5	45	15
Change in electricity use per teleworker (MWh)	–3.0	–3.3	–4.3	–3.5	–5.2	–3.5
Electricity savings (TWh)	–39	–62	–130	–78	–230	–52

The reduction in commercial floor space associated with telework is significantly greater than that associated with e-commerce in all scenarios. Telework's effect is particularly striking in Cybertopia, where high ICT usage among a dispersed population leads to more teleworkers who spend more days away from the office. For this scenario, telework brings savings of nearly 200 TWh in electricity use in 2021 compared with 2001, or more than 12 percent of Cybertopia's total 2021 commercial power consumption. In contrast, Zaibatsu's investments in intelligent transportation systems make commuting easier and result in less telework than in the Reference scenario. As a consequence, Zaibatsu's reduction in electricity use from telework in 2021, compared to that in 2001, is 39 TWh, or only about 2 percent of total consumption in the commercial sector.

4.3.5 Summing Up: ICT-Driven Commercial Electricity Use, 2001–2021

The combined effects on commercial power consumption of ICT equipment, EMSs, e-commerce, and telework are shown in Table 4.10 and Figure 4.7. To use 2001 as a baseline for comparing our projections with those in the *AEO 2002*, we assumed that our results for computer and telephone network equipment were included in the *AEO 2002* estimates for "other uses" and that our results for

---

percent/25 percent division of teleworking between the commercial and industrial sectors reflects the ratio of workers in each sector; see U.S. Census Bureau, 2001b.

Table 4.10

ICT Effects on Commercial Electricity Use, 2001–2021

| | | | Electricity Use (TWh) | | | |
| | | | 2021 Scenario | | | |
	2001	2006	Reference	Zaibatsu	Cybertopia	Net Insecurity
ICT equipment	92	115	178	196	148	219
Building EMS	–4	–31	–91	–100	–124	–77
E–commerce	–2	–7	–21	–25	–34	–10
Telework	–39	–62	–130	–78	–233	–52
ICT-driven subtotal	47	15	–64	–7	–243	81
Non-ICT subtotal[a]	1,120	1,250	1,650	1,650	1,650	1,650
Total commercial[a]	1,170	1,270	1,580	1,640	1,400	1,730
EIA total commercial[a]	1,170	1,340	1,840	1,840	1,840	1,840
Difference from EIA	0	–72	–257	–201	–347	–113
Difference from EIA as a %	0	–5	–14	–11	–24	–6

[a]Rounded to three significant figures.

EMSs, e-commerce, and telework were included in the *AEO 2002* estimates for space heating, space cooling, ventilation, and lighting. This makes our 2001 total match that of the *AEO 2002*, although the components differ in size: our ICT-driven component is much smaller than the one in the *AEO 2002*, and our non-ICT component is larger. For consistency with the *AEO 2002* projections beyond 2001, our non-ICT subtotal in future years increases at the same rate as the non-ICT subtotal in the *AEO 2002*.

The ICT-driven subtotal in Table 4.10 shows that in our projections for the Reference scenario, greater electricity consumption by ICT equipment in 2006 and 2021 is offset by usage decreases resulting from EMSs, e-commerce, and telework. The net effect is that our projected 2021 total electricity use by the commercial sector is 14 percent below that of the *AEO 2002*.[26] Cybertopia's increased energy management and telework cause its total to be 24 percent less than

---

[26]We used the *AEO 2002* average annual growth rate of 2.3 percent to extend the *AEO 2002* projected total for commercial electricity consumption from 1,800 TWh in 2020 to 1,840 TWh in 2021.

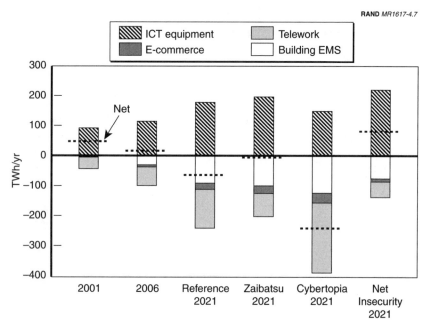

RAND *MR1617-4.7*

NOTE: Electricity savings (e.g., from EMSs) are shown as negative TWh/yr. The "net" lines show the sum of the negative and positive components for each year and scenario.

Figure 4.7—ICT-Driven Commercial Electricity Use, 2001–2021

the *AEO 2002's*, Net Insecurity's reduced telework brings its total closer to the EIA projection. As Figure 4.7 shows, electricity reductions from e-commerce are much less significant than those from energy management and telework in all four scenarios.

4.4 ELECTRICITY USE IN THE INDUSTRIAL SECTOR, 2001–2021

The industrial sector includes more than three million establishments engaged in manufacturing, construction, agriculture, forestry, fishing, and mining. The *AEO 2002* projects that industrial electricity consumption will increase at an average annual growth rate of 1.4 percent, from 1,023 TWh in 2001 to 1,416 TWh in 2020. The *AEO 2002* also projects that improved efficiencies throughout the sector will lower industrial electricity intensity (measured as kilowatt-hours consumed per dollar of output) about one-third from 2001 to 2020, taking it from 0.21 to 0.14 kWh/$ of output (EIA, 2001, Table 6).[27]

ICT's most significant applications in the industrial sector are to increase both production levels and productivity, primarily through better process controls. Throughout the 20th century, ICT use accompanied industrial electrification, which resulted in more electricity consumption along with vast improvements in output and productivity. But now that virtually all U.S. industrial production is electrically driven, the 21st century will see ICT applied to make production equipment and processes "smarter," which generally will translate into electricity savings (Commission on Engineering and Technical Systems, 1986, p. 116). As Huber and Mills (2001, p. 5) recently wrote:

> The old gear and pulley drives are rapidly being replaced with silicon driven power devices that allow manufacturers to cut more sharply, paint more finely and run a more reliable, more productive assembly line. Here again, energy efficiency will undoubtedly improve, so the transformation can be called conservation. But the change is a *conversion*, and it is impelled, first and foremost, by a quest for better performance.

According to the *1998 Manufacturing Energy Consumption Survey (MECS)* (EIA, 1998a), manufacturing represented more than 85 percent of purchased electricity in the industrial sector in 1998, and machine drives accounted for more than half of the power consumed in manufacturing.[28] Space conditioning and lighting used only 16 percent of the total electricity in manufacturing, compared with 33 percent and 50 percent, respectively, in the residential and commercial sectors. Thus, in addition to affecting building EMSs, e-commerce, and telework, ICT, when applied to machine drives and related process controls, can have a large impact on electricity consumption in manufacturing.[29] Other ICT applications, those using GPS location

---

[27]Output is measured in 1992 dollars.

[28]In addition to purchasing electricity, manufacturers generated 13 percent of the electricity they used.

[29]Some speculate that in the future (the time frame is generally unspecified), manufacturing instructions will be sent over ICT networks to production machines in

devices and networked sensors, are important to the mining, agriculture, forestry, and fishing components of the industrial sector.[30] Finally, increased use of ICT equipment throughout the economy generally implies the need for more electricity to manufacture the equipment.[31]

4.4.1 Industrial Electricity Use by ICT Equipment

Neither the *AEO 2002* nor the 1998 *MECS* breaks out industrial electricity use by computers and other ICT equipment, but Kawamoto et al. (2001) and Roth, Goldstein, and Kleinman (2002) include industrial office equipment in their power consumption estimates for 1999 and 2000, respectively. To develop a 2001 baseline estimate for the industrial sector, we started with the disaggregated data from Roth, Goldstein, and Kleinman and adjusted them to the industrial sector only, using the ratios of industrial/commercial electricity use by office equipment developed by Kawamoto et al. We then extrapolated to 2001 assuming a 4 percent growth rate. This process, which is similar to what we used for the commercial sector (see above), yields a 2001 baseline estimate of 13 TWh for electricity use by industrial office ICT equipment.

ICT sensors, processors, actuators, and transceivers are also embedded in growing numbers of industrial robots, machine drives, and other equipment used in industrial production and processes. Such industrial equipment is not classified as "ICT equipment," and we found no data on the electricity consumption of the ICT components

---

the home. "Someday, 'personal fabricators' will be used to make things like toy jeeps or wine glasses in the comfort of your own home" (Clancy and Rejeski, 2001). However, it is by no means clear that substituting home manufacturing for factory production would result in overall savings of electricity or other forms of energy.

[30]More-indirect effects of ICT on U.S. industrial sector electricity use include ICT-driven changes in the demand for industrial outputs (e.g., paper, compact disks, or other physical recording media) and ICT-facilitated outsourcing of industrial production offshore. For further discussion of possible substitutions of ICT network services for physical goods, see Romm, 1999, pp. 38–52.

[31]Although few data exist on this topic, Roth, Goldstein, and Kleinman (2002, p. 131) cite a Carnegie Mellon University estimate that 43 TWh were used to manufacture computers and office equipment in 1997. Estimating the changes in electricity needed for higher levels of ICT equipment manufacturing requires estimates of and/or assumptions about exports and imports, productivity improvements, and changes in the product mix of such equipment, which are beyond the scope of this study.

in this equipment. However, these ICT components use very little power, which means that even with an upper bound estimate of 50 million smart industrial machines continuously consuming an added 10 W per machine in 2001, their total incremental electricity use would be less than 5 TWh, or less than 0.5 percent of the industrial sector total. We assume 4 TWh for our 2001 baseline estimate, which is probably high.

For the Reference scenario, we project that electricity use by office ICT equipment will increase by about 2 percent per year, a rate similar to that for commercial sector office equipment. Consumption by the ICT components of production equipment will grow at a faster rate through 2010, but will then flatten as smart machines become the norm throughout the sector. Total power consumption by ICT equipment will remain less than 3 percent of the 2021 industrial sector total in all four scenarios.

4.4.2 Changes in Electricity Consumption from ICT Process Control

In contrast to our projection of a small increase in electricity consumption by the ICT equipment itself, we project large electricity savings from the improved control of industrial processes that ICT makes possible. Applications include better control of process heat, refrigeration, compressed air and steam systems, and (especially) motors and machine drives that represent more than 50 percent of industrial power consumption. Digital controls on machine drives continuously adjust motor speeds to follow loads more closely and thereby improve production quality. Adjustable speed motors also increase operating efficiency and reduce standby and operating power consumption; but it is improved quality and overall productivity, rather than energy savings, that drive their installation.

Our projections assume that adjustable speed motors improve machine drive efficiency by an average of 10 percent in 2001 and 20 percent in 2021 (Consortium for Electric Infrastructure to Support a Digital Society, 2001b, p. 15); and that in the Reference scenario, their penetration increases from 10 percent of industrial machine drives in 2001 (EIA, 1998b) to 40 percent in 2021. Because of the greater efficiency of adjustable speed motors, the percentage of industrial power consumed by machine drives decreases from 51 percent in 2001 to 49 percent in 2021. Total electricity savings in 2021 are 56 TWh in both the Reference and the Net Insecurity scenarios. Penetration of adjustable speed drives in 2021 is greater in Zaibatsu (45 percent) and Cybertopia (50 percent) than in the Reference case, leading to greater electricity savings—63 and 70 TWh, respectively—in these higher-ICT-use scenarios.

4.4.3 Electricity Savings from ICT-Facilitated Energy Management in Industrial Buildings

According to the *1998 MECS* (EIA, 1998b), 11 percent of manufacturing establishments had installed energy efficiency equipment that affected space conditioning and lighting. Using this figure as a base, we followed the process we used for commercial buildings (see Subsection 4.3.2) to project electricity savings from EMSs in industrial buildings (Table 4.11). The savings in 2021 range from 22 TWh (Reference and Net Insecurity) to 25 TWh (Zaibatsu) to 29 TWh (Cybertopia). All are considerably below the comparable estimates for commercial buildings, because the industrial sector uses far less electricity for space conditioning and lighting than does the commercial sector.

Table 4.11

Electricity Savings from Industrial Building Energy Management, 2001–2021

			2021 Scenario			
	2001	2006	Reference	Zaibatsu	Cybertopia	Net Insecurity
Buildings with EMS (%)						
Phase 1 (6% savings)	10	15	20	20	15	15
Phase 2 (16% savings)	1	10	20	20	25	20
Phase 3 (24% savings)	0	5	25	30	40	25
Total EMS buildings (%)	11	30	65	70	80	60
Electricity savings (TWh)	−1.2	−6.7	−22	−25	−29	−22

4.4.4   Changes in Industrial Electricity Use from E-Commerce

E-commerce's largest effects on electricity consumption are floor space reductions for retail stores and warehouses and power increases for data centers, both of which are counted in the commercial sector (see Subsection 4.3.3). However, B2B e-commerce and ITC-facilitated supply chain management can also reduce the amount of finished inventory needed per dollar of sales, which in turn can reduce the industrial sector electricity required to produce that inventory.[32]

In 1998, Ernst & Young estimated that e-commerce has the potential to reduce U.S. inventory levels by $250 to $350 billion, or 25 to 35 percent (Margeherio et al., 1998, p. 16).[33] Although this estimate seems overoptimistic to us, we used the 35 percent figure for Cybertopia, along with estimates of 20, 25, and 15 percent, respectively, in the Reference, Zaibatsu, and Net Insecurity scenarios. Our scenarios also use the *AEO 2002* (EIA, 2001) projections that, from 2001 to 2021, industrial sales will increase 75 percent in constant dollars, and electricity intensity (terawatt-hours per billion dollars of output) will fall 50 percent. The results (Table 4.12) show electricity savings from re-

Table 4.12

Changes in Industrial Electricity Use from E-Commerce, 2001–2021

			2021 Scenario			
	2001	2006	Reference	Zaibatsu	Cybertopia	Net Insecurity
Online sales (%)	5	20	70	75	80	60
Inventory saved with online sales (%)	10	15	20	25	35	20
Change in electricity consumption (TWh)	–1.1	–6.9	–34	–49	–59	–29

---

[32]Industrial inventories in 2001 were valued at about $1 trillion. See Bureau of Economic Analysis, 2001.

[33]This estimate has subsequently been widely quoted; for example, see Romm, 1999, p. 51; and OECD, 1999, p. 63.

duced inventory levels in 2021 ranging from 2 percent (29 TWh) of total sector consumption (Net Insecurity) to 4 percent (59 TWh (Cybertopia).

4.4.5   Changes in Industrial Electricity Use from Telework

Our analysis of the changes in electricity consumption that will result from telework in the industrial sector follows the analysis we used for the commercial sector (see Subsection 4.3.4). As in the earlier analysis, we estimate that 25 percent of teleworkers in each scenario are in the industrial sector, thus arriving at the results shown in Table 4.13.

4.4.6   Summing Up: ICT-Driven Industrial Electricity Use, 2001–2021

Table 4.14 and Figure 4.8 show the combined effects on industrial power consumption of ICT equipment, digital process controls, building EMSs, e-commerce, and telework. As with the residential and commercial sectors, for 2001 we matched our total to that in the *AEO 2002* to provide a baseline for comparison of projections in subsequent years. We also matched our non-ICT subtotal's rate of increase to that in the *AEO 2002*.

Because power consumption by ICT equipment itself is small in the industrial sector, greater ICT use lowers total electricity consumption in all four scenarios. Digital process controls, building EMSs, e-commerce, and telework all yield significant electricity savings. Total sector consumption in the 2021 Reference case is 112

Table 4.13

Changes in Industrial Electricity Use from Telework, 2001–2021

			2021 Scenario			
	2001	2006	Reference	Zaibatsu	Cybertopia	Net Insecurity
Teleworkers in sector (million)	4.3	6.3	10	7.5	15	10
Change in electricity use per teleworker (MWh)	−3.0	−3.3	−4.3	−3.5	−5.2	−3.5
Electricity savings (TWh)	−13	−21	−43	−26	−78	−17

Table 4.14

ICT Effects on Industrial Electricity Use, 2001–2021

| | | | Electricity Use (TWh) | | | |
| | | | | 2021 Scenario | | |
	2001	2006	Reference	Zaibatsu	Cybertopia	Net Insecurity
ICT equipment	17	21	35	38	38	35
Digital process controls	–8	–19	–56	–63	–70	–56
E–commerce inventory	–1	–7	–34	–49	–59	–29
Telework	–13	–21	–43	–26	–78	–17
Subtotal, ICT-driven	–6	–33	–121	–125	–198	–90
Subtotal, non-ICT[a]	1,030	1,140	1,450	1,450	1,450	1,450
Total industrial[a]	1,020	1,110	1,320	1,320	1,250	1,360
EIA total industrial[a]	1,020	1,130	1,440	1,440	1,440	1,440
Difference from EIA	0	–26	–112	–113	–186	–78
Difference from EIA as a %	0	–2	–8	–8	–13	–5

[a]Rounded to three significant figures.

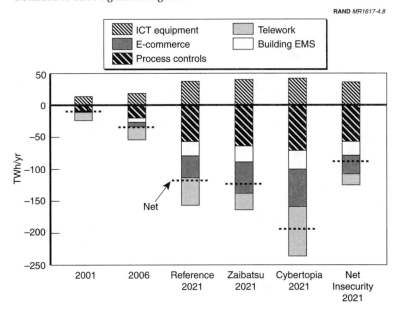

RAND MR1617-4.8

NOTE: Electricity savings (e.g., from EMSs) are shown as negative TWh/yr. The "net" lines show the sum of the negative and positive components for each year and scenario.

Figure 4.8—ICT-Driven Industrial Electricity Use, 2001–2021

TWh, or 8 percent, below that extrapolated from the *AEO 2002* projections. The projections for the other 2021 scenarios range from 5 to 13 percent below those of the *AEO 2002*. These results are similar to but smaller than those shown in Subsection 4.3.5 for the commercial sector.

4.5 PROJECTED ELECTRICITY USE IN THE RESIDENTIAL, COMMERCIAL, AND INDUSTRIAL SECTORS, 2001–2021

Table 4.15 and Figure 4.9 show our projections for ICT-driven and total electricity consumption in all three sectors. In the Reference scenario, the projected total in 2021 of 4,630 TWh is 346 TWh, or 7 percent, below the extrapolated *AEO 2002* projection.[34] Building

Table 4.15

ICT Effects on Residential, Commercial, and Industrial Electricity Use, 2001–2021

			Electricity Use (TWh)			
			2021 Scenario			
	2001	2006	Reference	Zaibatsu	Cybertopia	Net Insecurity
Computer, office, and network equipment	118	148	222	246	199	261
Other ICT equipment	79	98	184	190	193	206
Digital process controls	−8	−19	−56	−63	−70	−56
Building EMSs	−5	−40	−152	−170	−216	−124
E-commerce	−3	−14	−55	−75	−92	−40
Telework	−32	−53	−120	−72	−216	−48
Subtotal, ICT-driven	149	119	22	55	−203	200
Subtotal, non-ICT[a]	3,270	3,640	4,610	4,610	4,610	4,610
Total[a]	3,420	3,760	4,630	4,670	4,410	4,810
EIA total[a]	3,420	3,850	4,980	4,980	4,980	4,980
Difference from EIA	0	−89	−346	−311	−569	−166
Difference from EIA as a %	0	−2	−7	−6	−11	−3

[a]Rounded to three significant figures.

---

[34]We used the *AEO 2002* average annual growth rate of 1.8 percent to extend the *AEO 2002* projected total for electricity consumption from 4,880 TWh in 2020 to 4,980 TWh in 2021.

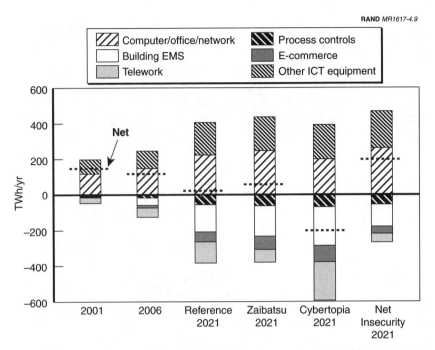

NOTE: Electricity savings (e.g., from EMSs) are shown as negative TWh/yr. The "net" lines show the sum of the negative and positive components for each year and scenario.

Figure 4.9—ICT-Driven Electricity Use in the Residential, Commercial, and Industrial Sectors, 2001–2021

EMSs and telework are responsible for the greatest electricity savings, with digital process controls and e-commerce also making substantial contributions.

Of the other three scenarios, Net Insecurity uses the most electricity in 2021 (4,810 TWh), primarily because the loss of trust in public networks results in lower power savings from EMSs, e-commerce, and telework. In contrast, Cybertopia's much higher use of EMSs, e-commerce, and telework leads to power usage that is 400 TWh less than that of Net Insecurity, or a total of 4,410 TWh. Zaibatsu's total, 4,670 TWh, is closer to that of the Reference scenario but reflects both greater power consumption by ICT equipment and greater savings from EMSs, e-commerce, and telework than does the Reference total. Figure 4.9 compares the relative importance of each component of ICT-driven electricity use within and among the scenarios.

A perhaps surprising outcome for an analysis based on future scenarios is that all four of our scenarios show lower total power consumption in 2021 than that projected in the *AEO 2002*, ranging from 3 percent lower (Net Insecurity) to 11 percent lower (Cybertopia). This difference stems principally from our baseline 2001 estimates for power use by computer, office, and network ICT equipment being more than 75 TWh, or 45 percent, below those in the *AEO 2002* (for the reasons discussed above, in Subsection 4.3.1). The difference widens to more than 200 TWh when projected forward to 2021.[35] If not for this systematic difference stemming from our lower baseline estimate, the 2021 projected electricity use for our Reference scenario would be only 2.5 percent lower (and for our Net Insecurity scenario, 1.3 percent higher) than that projected in the *AEO 2002*. In addition, the relatively narrow range of 400 TWh, or about 9 percent, between our lowest and highest projections for power use in 2021 reflects our assessment that ICT represents a roughly 5 to 6 percent factor in explaining total U.S. electricity consumption.

For the important category of computer, office, and network ICT equipment, our projections indicate relatively modest increases in power consumption over the 20-year period. Our 2001 estimate of 118 TWh represents 3.4 percent of total electricity use, which is consistent with the data in Roth, Goldstein, and Kleinman, 2002, and Kawamoto et al., 2001, from which our baseline was derived.[36] Looking forward, we see that greater power demands from larger numbers of more-powerful digital devices will be moderated by trends toward the use of more electricity-efficient components, low-power embedded devices, and wireless equipment and networks. Reflecting these offsetting trends, the 2021 Reference scenario projects that power consumption of computer, office, and network ICT

---

[35]The differences pertain to the residential and commercial sectors, since the *AEO 2002* does not estimate power use by computer, office, and network ICT equipment for the industrial sector.

[36]Roth, Goldstein, and Kleinman (2002, p. 3) estimate that computer, office, and network ICT equipment in the commercial and industrial sectors accounted for 3 percent of national electricity consumption in 2000. Including residential computers and home office equipment would add about 0.4 percent more to that estimate.

equipment will rise to 222 TWh, or 4.8 percent of total usage. Comparable projections for the Zaibatsu, Cybertopia, and Net Insecurity scenarios are 246 TWh (5.3 percent), 199 TWh (4.5 percent), and 261 TWh (5.4 percent), respectively.

Table 4.15 also shows power usage projections for other ICT equipment, which includes residential audio and video systems, home networks, and the ICT portion of industrial production equipment. Home audio and video systems, the largest components in this category, are today mostly analog devices whose power reliability requirements are different from and considerably less stringent than those for computers and other digital equipment. Over the next 20 years, however, audio and video equipment essentially will become all-digital and connected to digital home networks. Although home audio and video systems do not demand the same level of power quality and reliability (PQR) as do data centers and other mission-critical business systems,[37] they represent another component of electricity requirements for digital ICT equipment in an increasingly digital society.

From the perspective of total kilowatt-hours consumed, we find that very large increases in the number of digital devices and in the use of digital networks over the next 20 years will only modestly increase the demand for electricity. What will keep the increase in demand modest is primarily the use of ICT equipment that is more energy efficient, the growth of wireless systems, and the other offsetting trends discussed in this chapter. We looked for, but did not find, a set of plausible assumptions that might support a fifth scenario, one with ICT networks, computers, and office equipment using 10 percent or more of the national electricity total by 2021.[38] In none of our 2021 scenarios does this percentage exceed 5.5 percent. However, the rapid growth of ICT networks and equipment will dramatically increase the demand for high-quality and high-reliability power, which we explore in the next chapter.

---

[37]Jonathan Koomey, LBNL, private communication, 2002.

[38]We also did not include a "radical transformation" scenario in which greater efficiency, energy conservation, and lifestyle changes reduce ICT network and equipment use to below 3 percent of the national total. While plausible from a technological standpoint, such a scenario would require large-scale behavioral changes that are not supported by current studies or data.

Our analysis also led to several additional findings that seem reasonably robust across the scenarios:

*   Telework and ICT-facilitated energy management can have large effects on electricity consumption;

*   Both expanded use of digital process controls in manufacturing and B2B e-commerce bring power savings that are not as large as those for telework and EMSs but that are more consistent among scenarios with quite different assumptions;

*   B2C e-commerce has smaller effects on overall electricity consumption;

*   The power-saving effects of EMSs in the residential sector depend less on ICT advances than on consumers' behavioral responses to time-of-use and real-time pricing, which today seem highly uncertain;

*   Telework increases electricity consumption in the residential sector and lowers it in the commercial and industrial sectors, the net effect depending on both the number of teleworkers and the average number of days spent teleworking.

All our projections are, of course, rough estimates based on incomplete data and numerous assumptions about how the future might unfold. Nonetheless, further efforts to reduce uncertainties surrounding the factors identified above should help improve electricity demand projections made by the EIA and other, both public and private, forecasters.

Chapter Five

IMPLICATIONS OF THE SCENARIOS FOR THE U.S. ELECTRICITY SYSTEM

In addition to providing quantitative projections of electricity use, our analysis of the ICT scenarios identified four cross-cutting electricity supply issues that are of key importance:

- Assuring power quality for very large numbers of digital devices;

- Using ICT to improve grid reliability and operations;

- Using ICT to support distributed generation and storage;

- Reducing the vulnerability of the ICT and electricity infrastructures.

This chapter discusses each of these issues in turn. We consider how each plays out in the different ICT scenarios, what unresolved questions and uncertainties remain, and what the possible implications are for the EERE and other DOE energy supply programs.

5.1 ASSURING POWER QUALITY AND RELIABILITY FOR DIGITAL DEVICES

Throughout most of the 20th century, electricity was used primarily to power lights and motors. These analog devices are generally tolerant to voltage spikes and sags that can occur when large loads turn on or off, when a generating plant shuts down, or when natural events (e.g., lightning) or accidents disrupt the electric power grid. Because light-bulb filaments are fundamentally resistors and motors have heavy magnetic coils, both either dim or coast through short voltage fluctuations, resuming normal operation without serious problems once power is restored.

The generation, transmission, and distribution facilities making up the U.S. electricity grid were designed for such conventional analog loads. The grid delivers power with about 99.9 percent reliability—"three nines," in current parlance. This means that electricity users experience outages averaging a total of about eight hours per year, an amount that historically has been acceptable to most utility rate-payers. Hospitals and other essential facilities that cannot tolerate this level of outage install their own emergency generators or other standby power sources.

Digital devices demand higher levels of power quality and reliability (PQR),[1] as anyone can attest who has had to reset the household's digital clocks after a minor power interruption. This need for higher PQR stems from the fact that digital components require low-voltage direct current and are highly sensitive to short power interruptions, voltage surges and sags, harmonics, and other waveform distortions (Borbely, 2000). The increased sensitivity to PQR means that traditional levels of reliability may result in digital electronics, systems, and services shutting down when such problems occur. The important measure for digital technologies is the "downtime" rather than the "outage time," that is reflected by the conventional "number of nines" terminology.

End users differ as to how much downtime they experience from different kinds of power outages even when average outage time is the same (e.g., an average of eight hours per year under a regime of three nines reliability). For example, a supermarket that relies on freezers can tolerate many short outages much more easily than a single long one. In contrast, a semiconductor fabrication facility might find such short outages much more disruptive and costly than a single eight-hour power interruption. Thus, the traditional metric of reliability—the number of nines—is of limited value in under-

---

[1]Power *quality* is measured by amplitude fluctuations and deviations from a pure sinusoidal ac or constant dc waveform; power *reliability* depends on the frequency and duration of power outages. Both are critical for digital equipment. The Information Technology Industry Council (n.d.) has developed a "voltage tolerance envelope" that displays graphically the range of fluctuation and duration that most digital devices can tolerate without significant malfunction or damage.

standing the implications for digital technologies. Despite its drawbacks, however, the number of nines is still the metric used most often to discuss electricity reliability.

The need for higher PQR has led designers of some consumer digital products to include electrical storage (usually capacitors on circuit boards and/or backup batteries) to let the devices ride through short power interruptions and to smooth out voltage fluctuations. In addition, computer users are advised to purchase and install uninterruptible power supplies (UPSs) (which contain backup batteries, rectifiers/chargers, and inverters) to protect their machines from power line fluctuations that can damage sensitive components. Taking these steps can increase the effective reliability at the device level to five or six nines, equivalent to between a few minutes and 30 seconds of outage per year (Douglas, 2000).[2]

As ICT devices proliferate throughout the U.S. economy and society in the next two decades, more firms and individual households will require PQR at this higher level. Households will need high PQR not only for their computer and home office equipment, but also for their digital video and audio systems, home networks, and appliances with digital controls.[3] However, as discussed further below, the U.S. electricity transmission and distribution grid will be hard pressed to deliver reliability of more than three or at most four nines to end users. As a consequence, UPSs for home and business ICT equipment will become essentially ubiquitous.

Even the high level of PQR attainable through standard UPSs will be inadequate for commercial and industrial firms whose businesses depend on keeping their digital equipment operating nonstop. These businesses today include (among others) telecommunications operators, Internet service providers, and operators of Internet data centers or server farms; financial markets, credit card processors, and many financial service firms; Web service providers and other e-

---

[2]Again, the *downtime* resulting from outages is much more important than the total or average *outage* time.

[3]Refrigerators, washing machines, ovens, and other appliances will still need only conventional, three nines PQR for the motors, heaters, and condensers that constitute the bulk of their power load; but their digital controls and network interface devices will require a higher PQR level.

commerce companies; and semiconductor fabricators and other manufacturers using continuous, digitally controlled processes. Such "ultra-high PQR" users must invest not only in industrial-strength UPSs, backup generation, and storage equipment, but also in fast switching devices able to deliver backup power within a fraction of a 60-cycle electrical waveform—i.e., within a few milliseconds. Ultra-high PQR customers are particularly important to the evolution of a digital society because of the economic value of the goods and services they produce, rather than because of the number of kilowatt-hours they purchase.[4]

Our scenarios *assume* that ultra-high PQR is available to support the businesses that require it, albeit in different ways:

- In Zaibatsu, large vertically integrated utilities operate premium "power parks" and otherwise offer ultra-high PQR at premium prices to their digital customers.

- In Cybertopia, ultra-high PQR is widely available from distributed generators and local microgrids.

- In the Reference scenario, a mix of centralized utilities and distributed generators supply ultra-high PQR to end users that need it.

- In Net Insecurity (which requires the least ultra-high PQR of the scenarios), large organizations that need PQR produce their own or buy it from specialized providers. Most others—e.g., households and small businesses, which cannot afford the expense—find their ICT growth constrained.

From an energy supply viewpoint, however, the paths to assuring ubiquitous high PQR and rapidly growing ultra-high PQR in these scenarios remain unclear. PQR improvements can be made at several scales and levels: chip, device, power outlet, office or floor, building, plant, substation, or power park;[5] complex tradeoffs are involved in allocating costs and benefits at each level. At present, having the end user install UPS equipment for every sensitive digital device repre-

---

[4]We thank Jonathan Koomey, LBNL, for contributing this insight.

[5]In the premium power park concept, a utility or other electricity supplier guarantees high PQR, at higher rates, to tenants of a commercial office or industrial park.

sents a default solution. But projecting this solution forward to a time when there will be vastly greater numbers of ICT devices appears quite inefficient in both economic and energy terms. One need only observe the number of tangled cords, transformers, and UPS devices under today's office desks to appreciate the growing standby-power consumption problem accompanying increased use of ICT equipment.

Power conditioning that is built in at the chip or ICT device level would appear to have many advantages over separate UPS equipment. Redesigning chips to use lower voltages, a technology trend well under way, provides the opportunity to add PQR features. However, manufacturers of digital equipment may well underinvest in PQR, primarily because it would increase the cost of their products in highly competitive markets whose customers have not yet shown a willingness to pay extra for better power conditioning.[6] In addition, some common device-level components, such as switch-mode power supplies used for ac/dc conversion, are inherently nonlinear and introduce harmonic currents that can cause problems for other digital equipment.

At a larger scale, some power equipment manufacturers and distribution utilities propose developing premium power parks that guarantee high PQR to commercial and industrial businesses with sensitive digital loads. In 1999, EPRI (1999b) funded Siemens Power Transmission and Distribution and American Electric Power to conduct a demonstration power-park project in an existing industrial park in Ohio. Other industry stakeholders have also expressed interest, but the level of commitment to the power-park concept in a time of industry restructuring remains to be seen. More generally, deregulation and restructuring have blurred industry responsibility both for R&D and for ongoing investment in PQR. Although the industry places high priority on R&D for PQR,[7] both project funding and outcomes remain uncertain.

---

[6]Interview with industry executive, May 14, 2001. Some manufacturers may also view surge protectors or UPS attachments as attractive aftermarkets.

[7]For example, see EPRI, 1999a; and Consortium for Electric Infrastructure to Support a Digital Society, 2001b.

We cannot conclude that market failures in supplying high and ultra-high PQR really will constrain the evolution toward a digital economy, but we do question whether the current U.S. commitment to PQR R&D is sufficient to sustain the ICT growth projected in the Zaibatsu and Cybertopia scenarios. We thus suggest some possibilities that EERE and DOE might consider:

- Including PQR explicitly in technology program goals and plans;

- Assessing systemwide PQR issues, such as the cost-effectiveness of power conditioning at various scales and levels, and whether current investments in R&D by industry and government are likely to satisfy national requirements for PQR under plausible scenarios;

- Expanding R&D in areas found to be underfunded and critical to PQR—such as reducing harmonic distortions from switch-mode power supplies, adjustable speed motors, and other nonlinear ICT loads[8]—and improving high-capacity, fast-response, energy storage devices;[9]

- Informing industry stakeholders and end users about PQR problems and issues, as well as about technological and other approaches for resolving or mitigating them.

5.2 USING ICT TO IMPROVE GRID RELIABILITY AND OPERATIONS

The U.S. electricity transmission and distribution (T&D) system, much of which is many decades old, is showing increasing signs of stress as new and greater demands are placed upon it. Passage of the Energy Policy Act of 1992 required that access to utility transmission lines be opened in order to spur development of wholesale markets for electricity. The result has been a greatly increased volume of wholesale, or "wheeled," power transmission—by 1999, about 50

---

[8]See Borbely, 2000; and Waggoner, 2000.

[9]Storage technologies of interest include advanced batteries, flywheels, supercapacitors, and superconducting magnetic energy storage (SMES). See, for example, Gyuk, 2000, and other papers presented at the Electric Energy Storage and Technology Conference, Orlando, FL, September 18–20.

percent of all power generated in the United States (Douglas, 1999)—which challenges the operating stability of many transmission lines and the processes used to operate and manage them. At the same time, environmental concerns and local opposition make the process of building new transmission lines or increasing the capacity of existing ones long and arduous. Electricity distribution faces similar siting problems, as well as new, concentrated demands for high-quality power from Internet data centers and other digital loads. And the utility owners of T&D facilities may be reluctant to make new investments because of the uncertainties in revenues and returns introduced by industry restructuring.

ICTs show great promise for increasing T&D reliability and carrying capacity, but these advances are only beginning to move from development and field testing into operational use. As a consequence, our 2001–2006 common scenario projects that increased loading of aging facilities will result in more transmission congestion and a decrease in T&D reliability. This is then followed by grid improvements that take different forms in each 2006–2021 scenario:

- In Zaibatsu, heavy ICT investment and collaboration among the large, vertically integrated utilities leads to a unified, high-capacity, centrally controlled national grid and highly automated local and regional distribution grids.

- In Cybertopia, the technology supports efficient competitive markets for power and allows distributed control of, and widespread power exchange among, distributed generators and local microgrids. However, even Cybertopia needs a reliable national grid interconnected with the local microgrids.

- In the Reference scenario, ICT is used to support a mix of centralized and distributed grid controls.

- In Net Insecurity, large ICT investments are made to protect regional and local T&D grids from attack and to limit the spread of disturbances when they occur.

These ICT investments improve the overall reliability of the transmission networks to at least four nines and the distribution networks to three nines. It still costs too much to bring the entire grid up to higher levels, however, so digital equipment users buy premium power or have their own power conditioning to achieve high nines PQR.

Over the next two decades, ICT will provide the tools to monitor, measure, and assess grid performance in real time, route power flows, reduce loads, and take other measures needed to maintain grid stability and power throughput (Douglas, 1999; and Fairley, 2001). Developments under way include wide-bandgap semiconductors capable of handling high power flows; improved solid-state ac switches, controllers, inverters, ac/dc converters, and related components under the general rubric of power electronics;[10] high-temperature superconductivity (HTS) cables (Silberglitt, Ettedgui, and Hove, 2002); and better sensor and communication networks to detect and control disturbances on the grid (Amin, 1999).

ICT also will provide real-time information about electricity supply, delivery, and demand so that prices can be set more dynamically than they are today. The use of real-time pricing (RTP) to reduce peak loads and encourage efficient use of electricity—an approach much discussed by academics and energy analysts for many years— is now becoming feasible with the development and deployment of affordable digital meters and data links to businesses and homes.

All four of our scenarios posit that RTP will be generally available to end users by 2021 and that most commercial and industrial customers will have adopted it in their own economic self-interest. Residential customers are another matter. We remain unconvinced by the evidence to date that residential end users will change their behavior or automate their electricity consumption decisions simply because they have access to digital meters and RTP.[11] Their decisions will depend on the actual prices they pay, and it seems likely that, politically, consumers will be buffered from the highest peak rates imposed on business customers under RTP regimes. The scenarios thus depict different levels of consumer response: highest in Cybertopia, lowest in Net Insecurity.

---

[10]EPRI is supporting a number of power electronics development projects as part of its Flexible AC Transmission System (FACTS) program. See EPRI, 1999b, pp. 29–30.

[11]See Subsection 4.2.2 for discussion and references.

Other questions and uncertainties surround our assumptions that T&D equipment manufacturers and operators will in fact fund the R&D and subsequently make the ICT investments needed to improve grid reliability. Current R&D budgets for T&D are relatively small and continually under pressure as a result of industry deregulation. As a consequence, it remains unclear how soon the ICT developments supported under the Flexible AC Transmission System (FACTS), HTS, and other programs will become affordable to T&D operators and widely deployed. The Reference and Zaibatsu scenarios are particularly sensitive to such timetables, since they rely most on a high-capacity, reliable electricity grid to power greatly increased numbers of digital devices.

These points suggest two principal initiatives for EERE and DOE to consider:

- Assessment of systemwide T&D issues such as the economywide benefits and costs of greater grid reliability under different scenarios,[12] and whether current timetables are likely to be realized for the commercialization and deployment of FACTS, HTS, and related ICT developments;

- Expansion of R&D, in collaboration with industry stakeholders and with substantial cost sharing from industry, in areas found to be underfunded and critical to improving grid operations and reliability.

5.3 USING ICT TO SUPPORT DISTRIBUTED GENERATION AND STORAGE

Locating electricity generation and storage closer to end loads is likely to emerge as a major 21st century energy trend, reversing the trend toward larger-scale generating plants that guided electricity system development throughout most of the past 100 years. Up to

---

[12]The Consortium for Electric Infrastructure for a Digital Society (2001c) estimates that the current cost is $45.7 billion per year. Other estimates of annual losses to U.S. manufacturing firms from outages and power quality problems range from $25 to more than $150 billion (see, for example, SoftSwitching Technologies, n.d.). A new study under way at LBNL is reviewing the data and assumptions underlying these estimates; its findings should provide a better basis for future projections under different scenarios.

now, distributed generation (DG) units—mostly reciprocating engines fueled by diesel or natural gas—have been installed primarily for backup power, although there have been other applications as well, including peak-shaving and combined heat and power generation. DG units currently represent less than 1 percent of total U.S. generating capacity, but they nonetheless account for about one-third of U.S. power plants included in EIA databases.[13] Many DG installations also include distributed electrical storage in the form of batteries to provide immediate power before the generating unit kicks in.

Current technical and economic trends favor the growth of distributed generation and storage:

- DG technologies—internal combustion engines, microturbines, fuel cells, and photoelectric arrays—are well along in development and are becoming more cost competitive with technologies for centralized power plants;

- Locating DG close to the load can mitigate or avoid grid congestion, reduce T&D line losses, and produce heat that may be recoverable for cogeneration;

- DG and distributed storage can be combined with onsite power conditioning to deliver high nines PQR for digital loads;

- Greater concern about energy and infrastructure security increases the value of DG as a source of emergency or standby power.

Building on these trends, the DOE Office of Power Technology's strategic plan (Office of Power Technologies, 2000) has set an ambitious goal of increasing the share of new generating capacity represented by distributed energy resources from about 3 percent of annual additions in 2001 to 20 percent or more by 2010.

Our common 2001–2006 scenario projects that DG growth will increase to 10 percent of new capacity additions by 2006, which is

---

[13]The one-third estimate is based on analysis of operating and standby generating units included in the EIA's 860A and 860B utility and nonutility generator databases for 1999 (EIA, 1999).

consistent with OPT's strategic plan. Beyond 2006, the scenarios diverge in the following manner:

- In the Reference scenario, DG represents 30 percent of new generating capacity additions in 2021, with one-third of DG capacity regularly exporting power to the grid;

- In Zaibatsu, DG represents only 20 percent of annual capacity additions in 2021 and is largely owned and operated by the large Zaibatsu utilities, which integrate it with their centralized power plants and T&D networks;

- In Cybertopia, 50 percent of new generation capacity added in 2021 comes from DG, most of which is interconnected through local microgrids, and two-thirds of total DG capacity exports power to the grid;

- In Net Insecurity, DG represents 30 percent of new generating capacity in 2021, with little interconnection with or power exports to the grid.

In each scenario except Net Insecurity, a substantial portion of the DG installed after 2006 interconnects with and can export power to other users through local microgrids or the larger T&D network. Interconnection fundamentally changes DG's basic role from one of supplying backup power to a particular end user to that of providing economically dispatchable power as part of a fully distributed network. The ability to sell power, particularly during peak load periods, substantially improves DG economics and seems key to the rapid growth called for by its advocates.[14] This is the situation assumed in our Cybertopia scenario.

Many technical and nontechnical obstacles must be overcome, however, before DG installations and power sales take place on a large scale. The costs of microturbines, fuel cells, advanced capacitor storage, and other distributed energy technologies must continue to come down, and the operating performance of these technologies must improve. Reliability, longevity, and low emission profiles must be established for DG units that operate near-continuously rather than as backup. Technical standards must be developed for inter-

---

[14]For example, Dunn, 2001; and Silberman, 2001.

connecting large numbers of DG units to the grid without compromising safety or overall system reliability, and interconnected DG units must be able to respond to transient loads when exporting power. In addition, policies and methods for pricing DG power exports must be developed, and opposition by incumbent stakeholders, as well as current regulatory barriers to DG expansion, must be dealt with (Alderfer, Eldridge, and Starrs, 2000).

As with the larger grid, ICT plays an essential role in monitoring, analyzing, and controlling interconnected DG and distributed storage units. ICT is also needed to support real-time markets or other efficient markets for DG power sales. Although DOE, EPRI, equipment manufacturers, and software firms currently support R&D on such ICT developments, it is unclear whether the effort is sufficient to meet the needs for distributed power projected in our Reference and (especially) Cybertopia scenarios. We suggest in this case that EERE and DOE consider:

- Continuing to support development of DG interconnection standards;

- Supporting simulations and demonstrations of ICT systems for large-scale DG interconnection;

- Assessing systemwide issues such as overcoming the technical and nontechnical barriers to large-scale distributed resources, and whether current R&D investments by industry and government are likely to support DG growth under plausible scenarios;

- Expanding R&D in areas found to be underfunded and critical to the growth of distributed generation and storage;

- Informing industry stakeholders and end users about interconnection, personnel training, and other issues surrounding distributed generation and storage, as well as about technological and other approaches for dealing with them.

5.4 REDUCING VULNERABILITY OF ICT AND ELECTRICITY INFRASTRUCTURES

Whatever path it takes, the U.S. evolution toward a digital economy and society will bring greater dependency on always-available and reliable information, communications, and electricity networks (Ware, 1998). The ICT and electricity infrastructures already are intertwined and will become increasingly more so. Greater use of ICT equipment and services means greater need for reliable, high-quality power, and both traditional T&D networks and distributed microgrids will require real-time information, communications, and control.

The vulnerabilities of the ICT and electricity infrastructures to physical and information attacks were well recognized in a Presidential Commission report (President's Commission on Critical Infrastructure Protection, 1997)[15] published five years before the terrorist strikes of September 11, 2001, but the events of September 11 have accelerated efforts to improve infrastructure protection and resilience. High-priority R&D programs are aimed at designing more-robust architectures, hardening communication links, developing better sensor networks, improving data sharing and analysis to provide early warning of attacks, and mitigating damage from attacks. One important goal of this R&D is to come up with resilient, "self-healing" networks that largely automate system response to and recovery from natural disasters and human attacks (Amin, 2001).

Because such R&D efforts will take years and the results will possibly not be implemented for decades, and because attackers will continue to refine their methods and exploit new technology, our common 2001–2006 scenario estimates that the ICT and electricity infrastructures will face security and vulnerability issues in 2006 that are similar to those they face now. For the ensuing 15 years (through 2021), three of our four scenarios make more-optimistic projections, whereas the fourth does not:

- In Zaibatsu, the ICT and electricity grids become largely self-healing under centralized Zaibatsu control;

- In Cybertopia, distributed ICT and electricity resources develop self-healing properties, while local price signals help shed loads and limit losses after a failure or disruption;

---

[15]For the electricity sector response, see Working Group Forum on Critical Infrastructure Protection, 2001.

- In the Reference scenario, a mix of centralized and distributed controls make ICT and electricity infrastructures acceptably robust but not as self-healing or secure as in Zaibatsu or Cybertopia;

- In Net Insecurity, public infrastructures remain vulnerable, especially to information attacks, out through 2021.

The three optimistic scenarios assume that national, regional, and local electricity grids evolve to include secure networks of sensors, communication links, information processors, and dynamic algorithms that make the grids largely self-healing. However, the self-healing grid represents a concept and/or goal whose feasibility, cost, and timing are currently unclear. Similarly, the Cybertopia, Reference, and (to some extent) Zaibatsu scenarios assume that "virtual private networks" and/or the public Net provide communications with adequate security for both end-user load management and grid management functions. This assumption does not hold in the Net Insecurity scenario.

It is also important to note that while ICT advances support both centralized and decentralized scenarios, distributed resources add resilience and robustness to both the ICT and the electricity infrastructure. A recent paper by Balkovich and Anderson (2001) suggests that efforts to build redundancy in electricity and ICT networks be integrated at the neighborhood level. However, to our knowledge, the design tradeoffs between infrastructure robustness and overall system cost and efficiency remain largely unexplored.

We believe that our findings, new national priorities arising in the wake of September 11, and the essential public-good nature of efforts to reduce infrastructure vulnerabilities imply, in a reasonably straightforward manner, that EERE and DOE should consider

- Assessing the benefits and costs of spurring the growth of distributed resources as a strategy to increase infrastructure robustness, resilience, and flexibility;

- Analyzing efficiency/robustness tradeoffs for distributed resources and the T&D infrastructure;

- Assessing whether and how the Internet can be made secure enough for essential grid communications and control links, and supporting R&D on promising approaches;

- Expanding R&D on ICT developments for grid and microgrid monitoring, analysis, and control;

- Expanding R&D on ICT developments to encourage dynamic response by electricity end users.

Chapter Six

CONCLUSIONS AND RECOMMENDATIONS

6.1 ALIGNING EERE PROGRAMS AND PLANNING WITH ANTICIPATED ICT DEVELOPMENTS

While previous debate has focused largely on how much electricity will be needed to power the Internet and related information and communications technology (ICT) equipment, our analysis concludes that very large increases in the number of digital devices and network usage over the next 20 years will have only modest effects on overall U.S. consumption of kilowatt-hours. More important for a digital society will be meeting the increased demand for high power quality and reliability (PQR). We recommend that EERE explicitly include the improvement of power quality as a goal in its strategic plan and in appropriate R&D and technology programs.

A related conclusion of this study is that the electricity supply and distribution systems needed to support a digital society will increasingly rely on power electronics and other ICT developments for improved power measurement, monitoring, and control. These ICT advances are essential if PQR is to be improved for digital loads, grid reliability is to be increased, the growth of distributed energy resources is to be enabled, and electricity and ICT infrastructures are to be made more robust and resilient.

EERE may need to pay greater attention to accelerating the development of ICTs and their deployment into the U.S. electric power system. Our scenarios—especially the high-ICT-use Zaibatsu and Cybertopia—emphasize the importance of bringing the results of R&D into commercial practice to support the increased future demands of digital loads. In-time deployment of ICT in the electricity infrastructure depends on R&D success in reducing costs as well as in increasing performance. While EERE supports a number of projects in these areas, most of the relevant R&D is funded by industry. Electricity industry restructuring could lead to underinvestment in R&D and infrastructure improvements, although we cannot conclude that such possible market failures will seriously constrain ICT growth.

We recommend that EERE assess the goals, schedules, obstacles, and likely outcomes of current government and industry R&D programs in such areas as

- Power electronics for the transmission and distribution (T&D) system;
- Power sources for very small, wireless digital devices;[1]
- Energy storage for high-PQR applications;
- Self-healing microgrids and T&D networks.

If the analysis finds evidence for underinvestment, or for mismatches between likely availability and need, a good case can be made for supporting additional R&D or for providing incentives to deploy ICT in the electricity infrastructure.

To achieve its ambitious goals for distributed energy resources, EERE may also have to pay more attention to ICTs for monitoring and controlling the interconnection of distributed generation and storage units. We again recommend that EERE assess industry and government R&D to ascertain whether current efforts are likely to be sufficient. We specifically see a need to simulate and then physically demonstrate the technical and economic feasibility of interconnecting large numbers of distributed generation units that can export power during periods of peak load. As our Reference and Cybertopia scenarios show, ICTs are also important for supporting real-time or other efficient markets for distributed generation power sales.

---

[1]EERE's efforts here should be closely coordinated with those of DARPA, the primary government supporter of R&D on portable micropower sources. See Defense Advanced Research Projects Agency (n.d.).

Our Net Insecurity scenario shows most directly the added burdens and losses associated with continued infrastructure vulnerability, but improved infrastructure protection is important in each of the four scenarios. We recommend that EERE further explore how ICTs can support a larger role for distributed energy resources in reducing the vulnerability of the electricity infrastructure. Self-healing microgrids, secure communication links among distributed energy resources, and autonomous local agents for balancing electricity supply and demand—all of these deserve serious study and possibly increased R&D support. Given the increased national commitment to infrastructure protection and security since September 11, additional effort in this area could have a high payoff.

6.2 IMPROVING ELECTRICITY PROJECTIONS INVOLVING ICT

A digital society relies on high PQR. There is thus a need to better quantify and understand the dimensions of the so-called digital load—i.e., the portion of the electricity demand that, because it comes from ICT equipment and other applications, requires higher PQR than the conventional T&D grid now provides. In Chapter Five, we subdivide the digital load into two components with different PQR requirements:

- The *high-PQR load,* for most home and office computers, copiers, and other office equipment; digital television and audio systems; home networks; and the digital controls for growing numbers of networked sensors and appliances.

- The *ultra-high PQR load,* for network operators, financial service providers, e-commerce firms, semiconductor fabricators, and other businesses relying on digital ICT equipment that must operate continuously without interruption.

At present, no data are available for estimating either component of the digital load or for making sensible future projections. Consequently, we recommend that both EERE and EIA give high priority to efforts to collect such data and that EIA consider including estimates of the digital load as a separate category in the *Annual Energy Outlook.* Efforts to quantify the digital load, particularly its ultra-high PQR component, would also help inform government and industry decisions about new investments in the grid and in distributed energy resources.

EIA, EERE, and other offices within DOE should also give greater priority to ICT-driven electricity usage as part of the congressional mandate to make 20-year projections of U.S. electricity consumption in the *Annual Energy Outlook*. Based on our study, we recommend that additional analysis to improve projections of ICT-driven electricity consumption focus not only on the power directly used by digital equipment, but also on ICT influences on energy management and broader societal changes. The analysis presented in Chapter Four suggests specific topics deserving further study that includes actual measurements and projected trends:

- Telework in specific occupational categories and industry subsectors, including both the number of teleworkers and the average number of days spent teleworking;

- Effects of telework on electricity consumption in the residential, commercial, and industrial sectors, and on vehicle fuel consumption;

- Electricity savings from introducing adjustable speed drives and other digital controls in manufacturing processes;

- Inventory reductions resulting from business-to-business e-commerce;

- Warehouse and other commercial space reductions resulting from business-to-consumer e-commerce;

- Vehicle fuel savings resulting from business-to-consumer e-commerce;

- Consumer behavioral responses to time-of-use or real-time pricing of electricity;

- Effects of electric and fuel cell vehicles, in terms of both purchases of electricity for vehicle use and sales of electricity generated by these vehicles for other uses.

Each of these factors can have a significant impact on power use over a 20-year period, so better ways to estimate their effects can lead to improved overall projections of future U.S. electricity consumption.

6.3   IMPROVING ICT SCENARIOS FOR ENERGY PLANNING AND FORECASTING

This study should be considered an exploratory effort to create scenarios that illuminate potentially important ICT developments and to assess the implications of those developments for future electricity supply, demand, and delivery. We think that despite our need to rely on incomplete data and unprovable assumptions for the study, the process led to interesting and possibly useful findings, conclusions, and recommendations. Still, given the shortfalls and limitations, we think it essential to offer suggestions about how to extend and improve the process itself.

First, this study identified factors that were not explicitly included in the scenario building but that could be important to how ICT affects the U.S. electricity system. One of these driving factors is the extent of industry restructuring (in both the ICT and electricity industries). Another is any significant structural change in the U.S. industrial sector catalyzed by ICT developments—e.g., a decline in paper production as a new generation of readers substitutes digital interfaces for printed pages. Additional scenarios using these driving factors would help gauge their importance to and influence on ICT-driven changes in electricity use.

Second, another set of scenario excursions could draw on so-called "wild cards" that serve to challenge conventional assumptions and equilibrium solutions. Some examples of such low-probability, high-consequence events by 2021 are widespread chip-to-brain implants in humans, medical research definitively linking wireless ICT use with cancer, and networked, nanotechnology "personal fabricators" for on-demand manufacturing at home. Another, more plausible possibility is the use of large numbers of fuel-cell-powered vehicles as distributed generators of electricity when they are garaged or otherwise not in motion.

Finally, the ICT drivers could be further melded with demographic, cultural, and lifestyle variables to produce a more fully integrated set of future scenarios. This extension of the process would not be easy to accomplish, since adding more independent variables could quickly lead to an overload of scenario possibilities and choices. Nonetheless, scenarios that further integrate technical and nontechnical driving factors can provide a more complete framework for both DOE's strategic planning and its multiyear energy projections.

INFORMATION AND COMMUNICATIONS TECHNOLOGY SCENARIO MATRIX

Scenario	2001 Base	2006 Trend extrapolation from 2001	Reference 2021 Moderately high ICT use, balanced control
Demographics & GDP			
U.S. population	277 million	289 million	326 million
adult labor force	185 million	193 million	217 million
U.S. households	106 million	111.5 million	128 million
U.S. GDP (96$bn)	9,600	11,400	17,000
GDP per capita (96$)	34,700	39,400	52,100
Indust output (92$bn)	4,900	5,650	8,250
Basic technology			
processsors		Moore's Law (2x every 18 months) continues to hold	Moore's Law slows by 2015 to 2x every 4 years
storage		Moore's Law (2x every 18 months) continues to hold	Moore's Law slows by 2015 to 2x every 4 years
optical bandwidth	100 Gbps	DWDM bandwidth doubles every 1-2 years	bandwidth continues to double every 1-2 years
sensors		miniaturized (some MEMS), many networked	MEMS, some nanotechnology, many embedded
agents		useful in narrow domains	in general use
other artif. intel.		restricted to narrow domains	in general use, but doesn't replace human judgment
Voice recognition	niche uses	installed on high-end PCs and other devices	in general use
Biometric ID	experimental	used in secure systems and high-value transactions	in general use
MEMS	development	some industrial, medical, national security uses	widely used; some implanted for medical conditions
nanotechnology	research	in development	growing use in some industrial processes
implanted ICTs	research	in development; used with some prosthetics	widely used for prosthetics; some for augmentation

Scenario	2001 Base	2006 Trend extrapolation from 2001	Reference 2021 Moderately high ICT use, balanced control
Communications			
hh with telephone	94%	95%	95%; integrated with Net
adults w cell/PDA	30%	70%	90%
wireless systems cell/PDA equipment	2G (9.6Kbps)	2.5G deployed (64-128Kbps); 3G delayed new cell/PDAs have IPv6 addresses	4G systems widely deployed (5-20 Mbps) all devices have IPv6 addresses, software radios
cell/PDA equipment interoperability	pocket-size little	wearable devices becoming fashion items new devices connect to multiple protocols	devices built into clothing, jewelry devices interoperate with all wireless protocols
broadband wireless	little	802.1b networks in most cities, airports, hotels	largely integrated with 4G networks
digital broadcast TV	experimental	deployment delayed but available in large markets	available throughout U.S.; analog TV phased out
hh w cable or sat TV	75%	80%	95%; largely integrated with Internet TV
hh w digital TV	<1%	8% have digital TV; 60% have DVR/DVD player	98%; usually integrated with music systems
hh w interactive TV	<1%	15%	90%; largely integrated with Net
all-optical networks	in R&D	early commercial introduction	widely deployed
satellite comm apps		TV broadcast; low-orbit voice and data sys delayed	integrated with optical and wireless; remote sensing
fiber to curb/home	no	<5%	75%
Internet			
adults using Net	70%	90%	92%
computer in hh	52%	80%	95%, integrated or embedded
hh on Net	35%	70%	92%
broadband hh (256K)	9%	30%	90%
wireless Net access	<5%	35%; mostly low speed (<256K)	95%, integrated with other technologies

Scenario	2001 Base	2006 Trend extrapolation from 2001	Reference 2021 Moderately high ICT use, balanced control
broadband wireless	<1%	<10%	50%
infrastructure	overlay	some integration of telco, cable, wireless, Internet	full integration of telco, cable, wireless, Internet
backbone speed	100 Gbps	10 Tbps (terabits per second)	>1000 Tbps
address technology	IPv4	20% IPv6, driven by wireless devices	100% IPv6 or later version
networked PCs	100 million	150 million; growth now in non-PC devices	100-300 million; embedded devices often replace PCs
other Net devices	<25 million	300-500 million, driven by wireless services	4-6 billion or more, excluding home net devices
General applications			
e-mail	in wide use	still the most-used Internet application	integrated with voice and video communication
interactive games	starting	widely used, mostly by males	in general use
teleworkers, % (mil)	9% (17 mil)	13% (25 million)	18% (40 million)
avg days teleworked	2.0	2.1	2.5
videoconferencing	large orgs	used by businesses and many high-income consumers	in general use
E-commerce			
technology	early XML	XML well established	semantic standards spur automated transactions
software agents	primitive	assist humans in conducting transactions	conduct most transactions independently
B2B	EDI >50%	steady growth of SCM, auctions, sales on Net	nearly all transactions take place on Net
large firms using B2B	80%	90%	98%
B2C	1% of sales	growth resumes after B2C debacles in 2000-1	generally used, but retail stores still flourish
consumers using B2C	35%	55%	88%

Scenario	2001 Base	2006 Trend extrapolation from 2001	Reference 2021 Moderately high ICT use, balanced control
payment mechanisms	credit card	B2B largely automated; B2C = credit and debit cards	direct machine-to-machine transactions
security	SSL	PKI growth but not yet ubiquitous for B2C	biometric authentication not perfect but acceptable
taxation	moratorium	Congress working on unified federal/state taxation	VAT-like tax automatically included in transactions
Sector applications			
software		for business, largely outsourced and hosted on Net	seamlessly integrated with other Net offerings
software standards		open source increasing for business use	open source and proprietary each have ~50% share
entertainment			
movies		theaters starting to show electronic (not film) images	essentially all theaters show electronic images
virtual reality		various versions installed in theme parks, theaters	realistic but still distinct from real-world
distance learning		used by most college students, 30% of adults	integrated with on-site classes at all levels
health care			
medical devices		some smart devices linked to Net	MEMS implants for many chronic conditions
information on Net		used by ~25%; quality still highly variable	used routinely by patients before seeing physician
diagnostic software		used primarily for physician consults	used routinely by patients before seeing physician
remote monitoring		available for elderly and those with chronic problems	used routinely
telemedicine		used primarily for physician consults	used routinely to complement face-to-face visits

Scenario	2001 Base	2006 Trend extrapolation from 2001	Reference 2021 Moderately high ICT use, balanced control
transportation		>50% of new vehicles have GPS navigation systems 30% of new cars have embedded anti-theft IP chips	all post-2012 vehicles have embedded chips for ID, location, safety, road payments, "smart tagging"
Smart homes			
broadband networks		>10 Mbps built into 40% of new, 20% of old homes	in 90% of housing units
wireless networks appliances		generally available; takeup included in above Net-ready appliances available but not widely used	homes have integrated wireless/wired LANs all appliances have Net addresses
auto meter reading		built into most new units; 15% of total hh have it	used for all customers
energy mgmt systems real time pricing		<10% of homes have EMS based on RTP	70% have EMS with RTP; use varies
E-government			
gov't information taxes		clear trend to put public information online most tax filing, payments and refunds done online	esssentially all public information online automated tax payments on daily basis
local services		some use for obtaining permits, paying fines, etc.	generally done on Net
public safety		growth of Netcams for security	most public spaces monitored and shown on Net; auto theft greatly reduced by embedded ID chips
transportation-ITS		increased ITS investment but little payoff to date	widely deployed for traffic control, road payments

Scenario	2001 Base	2006 Trend extrapolation from 2001	Reference 2021 Moderately high ICT use, balanced control
environment		growth of Netcams for traffic monitoring California issues license plates with embedded chip growth of networked environmental sensors	Netcams generally on Net for traffic monitoring all post-2012 vehicles have embedded chips for ID networked sensors mandated at emission sites
e-voting	experimental	still experimental	feasible but still not widely used
Electricity applications			
power electronics		R&D lowers cost of fast thyristors	low-cost integrated power electronic chips developed
digital meters auto meter reading	<5%	installed in most businesses, 20% of homes feasible but utilities lag in implementation to homes	installed for all energy applications used for all customers
real-time pricing energy mgmt systems	<5%	widely available to businesses new EMS move from dedicated communications to Net	available to all customers EMS in general use
distrib generation		safety concerns resolved for DG interconnect to grid	feasible to interconnect large numbers of small DG units
storage		improved ICT controllers for flywheels, SMES	ICT controls for hydrogen storage
trans + distribution		FACTS devices begin deployment; R&D on HTS	HTS deployed; utilities offer dc power to ICT users
grid + control		Net-based alternatives to SCADA evolve	Net-based alternatives to SCADA in general use

Scenario	2001 Base	2006 Trend extrapolation from 2001	Reference 2021 Moderately high ICT use, "balanced control"
ICT issues			
competition		are proprietary "walled gardens" fragmenting Net? will software standards be proprietary or open? can Net backbone and ISP markets stay competitive?	are proprietary "walled gardens" fragmenting Net? will software standards be proprietary or open? can Net backbone and ISP markets stay competitive?
Digital divide		still an issue with ~30% of hh not yet on Net "broadband divide" a hot political issue	residual issue in U.S. (hot in developing countries) paying for increased bandwidth an issue for poor
Security		persistent problems of DDoS, malicious software most business e-mail encrypted firewalls installed by 50% of home users	problems still exist, but controlled; self-healing Net nearly all Net traffic encrypted all users have firewalls or equivalent (mostly) kept within acceptable limits
Cybercrime		ID theft growing; other kept within acceptable limits biometric databases under way for law enforcement ICT training no longer offered in prisons	biometric databases available for specific uses prison capacity reduced by continuous ICT monitoring
Privacy		many issues still unresolved	privacy sphere smaller than in 2001, but accepted
Intellectual property		many issues still unresolved	balance achieved; payments automated on Net

Scenario	2001 Base	2006 Trend extrapolation from 2001	Reference 2021 Moderately high ICT use, balanced control
Comments			scenario represents continuation of 2001 - 2006 trends, leading to moderately high ICT use and trust, somewhat more distributed control, but an overall balance between centralized and distributed control
Supporting refs		Computer Science and Telecommunications Board, 2001a	Computer Science and Telecommunications Board, 2001a

Scenario	Zaibatsu 2021 High ICT use, centralized control all entries as in Reference, unless noted	Cybertopia 2021 High ICT use, distributed control all entries as in Reference, unless noted	Net Insecurity 2021 Lower ICT use; fairly centralized all entries as in Reference, unless noted
Demographics & GDP			
U.S. population			
U.S. households			
GDP per capita (96$)			
Basic technology	faster ICT innovation and deployment	faster ICT innovation and deployment	slower ICT innovation and deployment
processsors			
storage			
optical bandwidth			
sensors		nanotech "smart dust" for env monitoring	
agents		agents make Net largely self-healing	
other AI			
Voice I/O			
Biometric ID			
MEMS			
nanotechnology			
implanted ICTs			
Communications	run by vertically integrated Zaibatsu	run by variety of large and small entities	run by large, still regulated firms
hh with telephone	98%—Zaibatsu give free basic accounts	98%	95%

Scenario	Zaibatsu 2021 — High ICT use, centralized control; all entries as in Reference, unless noted	Cybertopia 2021 — High ICT use, distributed control; all entries as in Reference, unless noted	Net Insecurity 2021 — Lower ICT use; fairly centralized; all entries as in Reference, unless noted
adults w cell/PDA	85%—more expensive than wired service	95%	90% have voice; 40% have data service
wireless systems	Zaibatsu deploy proprietary 4G systems		3G available, mostly used by business
cell/PDA equipment	proprietary; work best in Zaibatsu network	IP devices mostly used by business	
cell/PDA equipment interoperability	limited interoperability		limited interoperability mostly used by business
broadband wireless			
digital broadcast TV			
hh w cable or sat TV	95%	95%	98%
hh w digital TV	98%	98%	99%
hh w interactive TV	90%	90%	40%
all-optical networks			
satellite comm apps	emphasis on fiber optic over satellite	integrated; emphasis on remote sensing; earth's "electronic skin"	heavily used for digital TV to home
fiber to curb/home	85%—subsidized by gov't/Zaibatsu	65%—lower densities favor wireless	60%—no business case for non-Net users
Internet			
adults using Net	98%—Zaibatsu give free basic accounts	95%	80%—mostly using private Nets at work
computer in hh			
hh on Net	98%—Zaibatsu give free basic accounts	95%	50%—has declined from 80% in 2010

Scenario	Zaibatsu 2021 High ICT use, centralized control all entries as in Reference, unless noted	Cybertopia 2021 High ICT use, distributed control all entries as in Reference, unless noted	Net Insecurity 2021 Lower ICT use; fairly centralized all entries as in Reference, unless noted
broadband hh (256K)	96%	93%	45%
wireless Net access	75%—more expensive than wired service	95%	30%
broadband wireless	30%—more expensive than wired service	65%	25%
infrastructure	Zaibatsu have integrated "walled gardens"	wireless preferred, integrated with others	integrated to businesses, not to homes
backbone speed address technology	only within Zaibatsu networks		only within private networks
networked PCs			most hidden behind private firewalls
other Net devices	5-10 billion	15-25 billion, driven by wireless sensors	most hidden behind private firewalls
General applications			
e-mail	integrated within Zaibatsu network		widely used but not secure in public Net
interactive games	works best if all within Zaibatsu network		used by many but games often hacked
teleworkers, % (mil) avg days teleworked	14% (30 million); more rely on ITS 2.0	28% (60 million) 3.0	9% (20 million); most in large orgs 2.0
videoconferencing	works best if all within Zaibatsu network	even more widely used than in Reference	used within secure business Nets
E-commerce			
technology	mostly Zaibatsu proprietary		designed for secure B2B transactions

Scenario	Zaibatsu 2021 High ICT use, centralized control all entries as in Reference, unless noted	Cybertopia 2021 High ICT use, distributed control all entries as in Reference, unless noted	Net Insecurity 2021 Lower ICT use; fairly centralized all entries as in Reference, unless noted
software agents B2B	mostly Zaibatsu proprietary		used within secure private Nets only within secure private Nets
large firms using B2B	99%	98%	90%
B2C	incentives to buy within Zaibatsu group	more B2C substitution for retail stores	very low level due to security concerns
consumers using B2C	95%	95%	25%
payment mechanisms	incentives to buy within Zaibatsu group		multiple levels of authentication required
security	high security within Zaibatsu networks		ok within business nets; poor in public Net
taxation	national VAT automatically included		automated for B2B within business Nets
Sector applications			
software	seamless within Zaibatsu network		on business Nets; on DVD+ for home users
software standards	proprietary software dominates	open systems dominate	proprietary software dominates
entertainment movies			available at home via one-way media, DVD+
virtual reality	large Zaibatsu investment in VR for home		in theaters; some packaged VR for homes
distance learning	heavily marketed by Zaibatsu	very strong use in low density areas	most on business Nets; some on public Net
health care			
medical devices			

Scenario	Zaibatsu 2021 High ICT use, centralized control all entries as in Reference, unless noted	Cybertopia 2021 High ICT use, distributed control all entries as in Reference, unless noted	Net Insecurity 2021 Lower ICT use; fairly centralized all entries as in Reference, unless noted
information on Net			available on public Net but not trusted
diagnostic software remote monitoring			packaged software used at home in decline after false data led to deaths
telemedicine		very widely used in low density areas	used only within private medical Nets
transportation	even greater use of ICTs for work, entertainment while in ITS mode		
Smart homes broadband networks	in 95%; Zaibatsu subsidized	in 95%; mostly wireless	90% have networks; few connect to Net
wireless networks appliances			few on Net since hackers set homes on fire
auto meter reading			50% of homes, mostly via dedicated links
energy mgmt systems	Zaibatsu run EMSs for consumers	wide market for EMS services	all EMSs done within residence
E-government gov't information			available on public Net but not trusted
taxes			not automated; can be filed on secure Nets
local services	outsourced to Zaibatsu and done on Net	many business/gov't/NGO partnerships	in decline due to false info sent by hackers

Scenario	Zaibatsu 2021 High ICT use, centralized control all entries as in Reference, unless noted	Cybertopia 2021 High ICT use, distributed control all entries as in Reference, unless noted	Net Insecurity 2021 Lower ICT use; fairly centralized all entries as in Reference, unless noted
public safety			public Net Webcams vulnerable to spoofing
transportation-ITS	huge investment by Zaibatsu and gov't automated vehicle spacing, road payments greater use of embedded ICT	less investment in ITS	traffic Webcams no longer on public Net
environment	sensor data mostly for Zaibatsu and gov't	NGOs actively monitor data on Net	sensor data only on secure gov Nets
e-voting	implemented by Zaibatsu/gov't partnerships		no longer used due to e-voting vulnerability
Electricity applications			
power electronics	more emphasis on grid than DG apps	more emphasis on DG than grid apps	emphasis on DG and grid security
digital meters			
auto meter reading			
real-time pricing			
energy mgmt systems			
distrib generation			
storage			
trans + distribution			
grid + control			grid subject to constant hacker attacks

Scenario	Zaibatsu 2021 High ICT use, centralized control all entries as in Reference, unless noted	Cybertopia 2021 High ICT use, distributed control all entries as in Reference, unless noted	Net Insecurity 2021 Lower ICT use; fairly centralized all entries as in Reference, unless noted
ICT issues			
competition	Zaibatsu limit interconnection; proprietary software dominates; Zaibatsu have driven out other ISPs		business Nets competitive but cartelized; proprietary software dominates; public ISPs competitive but not profitable
digital divide	not really an issue in U.S.		gap is between private and public Net users
security	higher security within Zaibatsu networks		acceptable security within private Nets; trust in public Net in decline since 2012; gov't unable to stop non-U.S. hackers
cybercrime	harsh laws passed against cybercrime; more gov/Zaibatsu use of biometrics		massive ID theft despite harsh laws; biometric databases incomplete; spoofable; ICT monitoring of felons not reliable
privacy	very little privacy, but accepted by most	individual largely controls privacy sphere	those seeking privacy don't use public Net
intellectual property	Zaibatsu control most intellectual property		

	Zaibatsu 2021	Cybertopia 2021	Net Insecurity 2021
Scenario	High ICT use, centralized control — all entries as in Reference, unless noted	High ICT use, distributed control — all entries as in Reference, unless noted	Lower ICT use; fairly centralized — all entries as in Reference, unless noted
Comments	scenario emphasizes growth in cities and suburbs, wired over wireless infrastructure, ITS instead of telework, smart tags on physical goods, large ICT investments by Zaibatsu/gov't partnerships, active federal regulation, less state or local role	scenario emphasizes growth in lower density areas, wireless over wired infrastructure, more telework and B2C, very wide use of untethered sensors, ICT investments by business/NGO/gov't partnerships	scenario emphasizes loss of public trust in ICT networks due to unresolved security concerns. Secure, private Nets serve large organizations, but only 50% of hh connect to public Net. Heavy use of one-way media and stand-alone ICT devices
Supporting refs	Lessig, 1999; Air University, 1995	Glenn and Gordon, 2000	"Snowdrops" scenario in Botterman et al., 2001

Acronyms
(not otherwise defined in text)

DDoS	distributed denial of service	Mbps	Megabits per second
DVR	digital video recorder	PKI	Public Key Infrastructure
DWDM	dense wave division matrix	SCADA	Supervisory Control and Data Acquisition
EDI	electronic data interchange	SCM	supply chain management
Gbps	Gigabits per second	SMES	superconducting magnetic energy storage
GDP	Gross Domestic Product	SSL	secure socket link
ID	identification	Tbps	Terabits per second
IPv6	Internet Protocol version 6	VAT	Value-Added Tax
ITS	Intelligent Transportation System	XML	Extensible Markup Language
kbps	kilobits per second	2G, 3G, 4G	2nd, 3rd, 4th generation

ICT-RELATED ELECTRICITY USE PROJECTIONS

U.S. Residential		2001 Base				2006		
households (million)				106				111.5
electricity intensity (kWh/hh)				11,600				12,300
avg. sq. ft. per hh				1,684				1,713
ICT Equipment	% of hh	# units (million)	unit kWh/yr	TWh/yr	% of hh	# units (million)	unit kWh/yr	TWh/yr
Computer/office								
desktop		65	110	7.2		85	100	8.5
notebook		6	10	0.1		10	10	0.1
PDA (charger)		15	10	0.2		75	10	0.8
printer, other periph		90	20	1.8		120	20	2.4
modem		45	20	0.9	40	45	20	0.9
broadband modem		9	40	0.4	30	33	40	1.3
copier/fax		12	275	3.3	20	22	225	5.0
subtotal				13.7				19.0
(EIA 2001)				14.7				17.6
TV/video								
cable/sat TV/video	72	76	450	34.3	80	89	450	40.1
broadcast TV/video	27	29	350	10.0	19	21	350	7.4
digital TV (increm.)	1	1	180	0.2	5	6	180	1.0
dig cable/sat box	18	19	100	1.9	50	56	90	5.0
game console		65	10	0.7	100	112	10	1.1
subtotal				47.1				54.7
(EIA, 2001)				41.0				52.7
Audio								
component stereo		75	150	11.3	70	78	150	11.7
compact stereo		50	110	5.5	50	56	110	6.1
portable stereo		75	17	1.3	75	84	17	1.4
clock radio		150	15	2.3	150	167	15	2.5
MP3 player		5	10	0.1	50	56	10	0.6
subtotal				20.3				22.3
Communications/network								
powered phone/ans		100	26	2.6		100	26	2.6
cordless phone/ans		100	30	3.0		150	30	4.5
cell phone charger		40	10	0.4		75	10	0.8
home network-base	3	3	100	0.3	20	22	100	2.2
security sys/connect	12	13	125	1.6	30	446	2.25	2.4
ICT connections		10	2.75	0.0		223	2.25	0.5
appliance connects		0	2.75	0.0		45	2.25	0.1
HVAC/light connects		2	2.75	0.0		223	2.25	0.5
subtotal				7.9				13.6
Subtotal ICT equipment				89				110

U.S. Residential	2001 Base				2006			
households (million)				106				111.5
electricity intensity (kWh/hh)				11,600				12,300
avg. sq. ft. per hh				1,684				1,713
ICT Equipment	% of hh	# units (million)	unit kWh/yr	TWh/yr	% of hh	# units (million)	unit kWh/yr	TWh/yr
Home EMS	% SP[a]	% pene- tration	% SC&L[b]		% SP[a]	% pene- tration	% SC&L[b]	
phase 1	3	2	34	−0.3	3	7	34	−1.0
phase 2	9	0	34	0.0	9	2	34	−0.8
phase 3	15	0	34	0.0	15	1	34	−0.7
subtotal EMS				−0.3				−2.5
Telework								
% of work force	9%	17			13%	25		
avg days per week	2				2.1			
office equip (increm)		17	220	3.0		25	210	4.4
office lighting		17	150	2.0		25	140	2.9
office space conditioning		17	500	6.8		25	500	10.5
subtotal home office		17	870	11.8		25	850	17.9
rest of home (2/3 x office)		17	580	7.9		25	567	11.9
subtotal telework		1,450		19.7		1,417		29.8
subtotal ICT-driven				109				137
subtotal non-ICT				1,121				1,241
Total residential				1,230				1,378
EIA ICT				56				70
EIA non-ICT				1,174				1,300
EIA total residential				1,230				1,370
difference from EIA								
TWh				0				8
%				0.0				0.6

References and sources of data:
EIA, 2001
Arrington, 2001
Kawamoto et al., 2001
Rosen and Meier, 1999
Rosen and Meier, 2000
Rosen, Meier, and Zandelin, 2001

[a]SP = savings potential.
[b]SC&L = space conditioning and lighting.

U.S. Residential	Reference 2021				Zaibatsu 2021			
households (million)				128				
electricity intensity (kWh/hh)				13,200				
avg. sq. ft. per hh				1,792				
ICT Equipment	% of hh	# units (million)	unit kWh/yr	TWh/yr	% of hh	# units (million)	unit kWh/yr	TWh/yr
Computer/office								
desktop		100	100	10.0		120	100	12.0
notebook		25	10	0.3		30	10	0.3
PDA (charger)		150	10	1.5		150	10	1.5
printer, other periph		150	20	3.0		160	20	3.2
modem	2	3	20	0.1	2	3	20	0.1
broadband modem	90	115	40	4.6	96	123	40	4.9
copier/fax	30	38	150	5.8	35	45	150	6.7
subtotal				25.2				28.7
(EIA, 2001)				33.7				33.7
TV/video								
cable/sat TV+video	95	122	450	54.7	98	125	450	56.4
other TV/video	4	5	350	1.8	1	1	350	0.4
digital TV (add kWh)	95	122	180	21.9	98	125	180	22.6
dig cable/sat box	95	122	60	7.3	98	125	60	7.5
game console	150	192	10	1.9	150	192	10	1.9
subtotal				87.6				88.9
(EIA, 2001)				76.3				76.3
Audio								
component stereo	75	96	150	14.4	75	96	150	14.4
compact stereo	50	64	110	7.0	50	64	110	7.0
portable stereo	75	96	17	1.6	75	96	17	1.6
clock radio	150	192	15	2.9	150	192	15	2.9
MP3 player	150	192	10	1.9	150	192	10	1.9
subtotal				27.9				27.9
Communications/network								
powered phone/ans		100	26	2.6		110	28	3.1
cordless phone/ans		200	30	6.0		200	28	5.6
cell phone charger		30	10	0.3		25	10	0.3
home network-base	90	115	150	17.3	95	122	150	18.2
security sys/connect		3,456	1.34	4.6		3,648	1.34	4.9
ICT connections		3,456	1.34	4.6		3,648	1.34	4.9
appliance connects		3,584	1.34	4.8		4,096	1.34	5.5
HVAC/light connects		8,960	1.34	12.0		10,240	1.34	13.7
subtotal				52.3				56.2
Subtotal ICT equipment				193				202

U.S. Residential		Reference 2021				Zaibatsu 2021		
households (million)			128					
electricity intensity (kWh/hh)			13,200					
avg. sq. ft. per hh			1792					
Item	% of hh	# units (million)	unit kWh/yr	TWh/yr	% of hh	# units (million)	unit kWh/yr	TWh/yr
Home EMS	% SP[a]	% penetration	% SC&L[b]		% SP[a]	% penetration	% SC&L[b]	
phase 1	3	20	33	−3.4	3	20	33	−3.4
phase 2	9	20	33	−10.1	9	25	33	−12.6
phase 3	15	30	33	−25.2	15	35	33	−29.5
subtotal EMS				−38.7				−45.4
Telework								
% of work force	18	40			14	30		
avg days per week	2.5				2			
office equip (increm)		40	180	7.2		30	180	4.3
office lighting		40	110	4.4		30	110	2.6
office space conditioning		40	500	20.0		30	500	12.0
subtotal home office		40	790	31.6		30	790	19.0
rest of home (2/3 x office)		40	527	21.1		30	527	12.6
subtotal telework			1,317	52.7		30	1,317	31.6
subtotal ICT-driven				207				188
subtotal non-ICT				1,516				1,516
Total residential				1,723				1,704
EIA ICT				113				113
EIA non-ICT				1,587				1,587
EIA total residential				1,700				1,700
difference from EIA								
TWh				23				4
%				1.3				0.2

[a]SP = savings potential.
[b]SC&L = space conditioning and lighting.

U.S. Residential households (million) electricity intensity (kWh/hh) avg. sq. ft. per hh	Cybertopia 2021				Net Insecurity 2021			
ICT Equipment	% of hh	# units (million)	unit kWh/yr	TWh/yr	% of hh	# units (million)	unit kWh/yr	TWh/yr
Computer/office								
desktop		120	100	12.0		100	100	10.0
notebook		30	10	0.3		25	10	0.3
PDA (charger)		200	10	2.0		50	10	0.5
printer, other periph		180	20	3.6		150	20	3.0
modem	2	3	20	0.1	2	3	20	0.1
broadband modem	93	119	40	4.8	50	64	40	2.6
copier/fax	40	51	150	7.7	30	38	150	5.8
subtotal				30.4				22.1
(EIA, 2001)				33.7				33.7
TV/video								
cable/sat TV+video	95	122	450	54.7	98	125	450	56.4
other TV/video	4	5	350	1.8	1	1	350	0.4
digital TV (add kWh)	98	125	180	22.6	99	127	400	50.7
dig cable/sat box	95	122	60	7.3	99	127	60	7.6
game console	150	192	10	1.9	170	218	10	2.2
subtotal				88.3				117.4
(EIA, 2001)				76.3				76.3
Audio								
component stereo	75	96	150	14.4	80	102	150	15.4
compact stereo	50	64	110	7.0	60	77	110	8.4
portable stereo	75	96	17	1.6	80	102	17	1.7
clock radio	150	192	15	2.9	150	192	15	2.9
MP3 player	150	192	10	1.9	150	192	10	1.9
subtotal				27.9				30.3
Communications/network								
powered phone/ans		100	28	2.8		100	28	2.8
cordless phone/ans		200	28	5.6		200	28	5.6
cell phone charger		30	10	0.3		30	10	0.3
home network-base	95	122	150	18.2	80	102	150	15.4
security connects		3,648	1.34	4.9		3,072	1.34	4.1
ICT connections		3,648	1.34	4.9		1,024	1.34	1.4
appliance connects		4,608	1.34	6.2		896	1.34	1.2
HVAC/light connects		11,520	1.34	15.4		8,960	1.34	12.0
subtotal				58.3				42.8
Subtotal ICT equipment				205				213

U.S. Residential households (million) electricity intensity (kWh/hh) avg. sq. ft. per hh Item	Cybertopia 2021				Net Insecurity 2021			
	% of hh	# units (million)	unit kWh/yr	TWh/yr	% of hh	# units (million)	unit kWh/yr	TWh/yr
Home EMS	% SP[a]	% penetration	% SC&L[b]		% SP[a]	% penetration	% SC&L[b]	
phase 1	3	10	33	−1.7	3	40	33	−6.7
phase 2	9	20	33	−10.1	9	20	33	−10.1
phase 3	15	60	33	−50.5	15	10	33	−8.4
subtotal EMS				-62.3				−25.2
Telework								
% of work force	28	60			9	20		
avg days per week	3				2			
office equip (increm)		60	180	13.0		20	180	2.9
office lighting		60	110	7.9		20	110	1.8
office space conditioning		60	500	36.0		20	500	8.0
subtotal home office		60	790	56.9		20	790	12.6
rest of home (2/3 x office)		60	527	37.9		20	527	8.4
subtotal telework			1,317	94.8			1,317	21.1
subtotal ICT-driven				237				208
subtotal non-ICT				1,516				1,516
Total residential				1,753				1,724
EIA ICT				113				113
EIA non-ICT				1,587				1,587
EIA total residential				1,700				1,700
difference from EIA								
TWh				53				24
%				3.1				1.4

[a]SP = savings potential.
[b]SC&L = space conditioning and lighting.

U.S. Commercial	2001 Base				2006			
floor space (billion square feet)			66.1				72.9	
electricity intensity (kWh/sq ft)			17.7				18.4	
Item	# units (million)	unit kWh/yr	TWh/yr		# units (million)	unit kWh/yr	TWh/yr	
ICT equipment								
PC equipment	69 (PCs)	650	44.5		83 (PCs)	600	50.0	
other office ICT			28.8				35.0	
data centers	12M ft²	350	4.2		28M ft²	350	9.8	
FTTC, FTTH terminals	0	1,750	0.0		2	430	0.9	
other network ICT			14.0				19.0	
subtotal ICT equipment			91.5				114.7	
Building EMS	% SP[a]	% penetration	% SC&L[b]		% SP[a]	% penetration	% SC&L[b]	
phase 1	6	10	51	−3.6	6	20	48	−7.7
phase 2	16	0	51	0.0	16	15	48	−15.4
phase 3	24	0	51	0.0	24	5	48	−7.7
subtotal EMS				−3.6				−30.9
E-commerce	% online	% space saved	retail % of elec		% online	% space saved	retail % of elec	
B2C—retail space	2	50	14	−1.6	7	50	14	−5.5
			warehse % of elec				warehse % of elec	
B2B—warehouse sp	5	10	6.8	−0.4	20	10	6.8	−1.5
subtotal e-commerce				−1.9				−7.0
Telework	million	kWh/yr			million	kWh/yr		
number	9	12.8			13	18.8		
avg days per week	2				2.1			
electricity savings		−3,034	−38.7			−3,300	−61.9	
subtotal ICT-driven			47				15	
subtotal non-ICT			1,123				1,253	
Total commercial			1,170				1,268	
EIA ICT			152				204	
EIA non-ICT			1,018				1,136	
EIA total commercial			1,170				1,340	
difference from EIA								
TWH			0				−72	
%			0				−5	

References and data sources
CBECS, 1995
EIA, 2001
Kawamoto et al., 2001
Roth, Goldstein, and Kleinman, 2002
Mitchell-Jackson, 2001

[a]SP = savings potential.
[b]SC&L = space conditioning and lighting.

	Reference 2021				**Zaibatsu 2021**			
U.S. Commercial floorspace (billion sq ft)			91.1					
electricity intensity (kWh/sq ft)			20.2					
Item	**# units (million)**	**unit kWh/yr**		**TWh/yr**	**# units (million)**	**unit kWh/yr**		**TWh/yr**
ICT Equipment								
PC equipment				65.0				70.0
other office ICT				45.0				50.0
data centers	65M ft²	400		26.0	75M ft²	400		30.0
FTTC, FTTH terminals	96	100		9.6	110	100		11.0
other network ICT				32.0				35.0
subtotal ICT equipment				177.6				196.0
Building EMS	% SP[a]	% penetration	% SC&L[b]		% SP[a]	% penetration	% SC&L[b]	
phase 1	6	20	40	−8.8	6	20	40	−8.8
phase 2	16	25	40	−29.4	16	25	40	−29.4
phase 3	24	30	40	−53.0	24	35	40	−61.8
subtotal EMS				−91.3				−100.1
E-commerce	% online	% space saved	retail % of elec		% online	% space saved	retail % of elec	
B2C—retail space	20	50	14	−15.6	25	50	14	−19.5
			warehse % of elec				warehse % of elec	
B2B—warehouse sp	70	10	6.8	−5.4	75	10	6.8	−5.8
subtotal e-commerce				−21.0				−25.3
Telework	million	kWh/yr			million	kWh/yr		
number	18	30.0			14	22.5		
avg days per week	2.5				2			
electricity savings		−4,315		−129.5		−3,452		−77.7
subtotal ICT-driven				−64				−7
subtotal non-ICT				1,648				1,646
Total commercial				1,583				1,639
EIA ICT				346				346
EIA non-ICT				1,494				1,494
EIA total commercial				1,840				1,840
difference from EIA								
TWH				−257				−201
%				−14				−11

[a]SP = savings potential.

[b]SC&L = space conditioning and lighting.

U.S. Commercial	Cybertopia 2021			Net Insecurity 2021		
Item	# units (million)	unit kWh/yr	TWh/yr	# units (million)	unit kWh/yr	TWh/yr
ICT equipment						
PC equipment			50.0			90.0
other office ICT			40.0			70.0
data centers	50M ft²	400	20.0	45M ft²		18.0
FTTC, FTTH terminals	83	100	8.3	64	100	6.4
other network ICT			30.0			35.0
subtotal ICT equipment			148.3			219.4
Building EMS	% SP[a]	% penetration	% SC&L[b]	% SP[a]	% penetration	% SC&L[b]
phase 1	6	15	40 −6.6	6	20	40 −8.8
phase 2	16	25	40 −29.4	16	20	40 −23.6
phase 3	24	50	40 −88.3	24	25	40 −44.2
subtotal EMS			−124.4			−76.5
E-commerce	% online	% space saved	retail % of elec	% online	% space saved	retail % of elec
B2C—retail space	35	50	14 −27.3	7	50	14 −5.5
			warehse % of elec			warehse % of elec
B2B—warehouse sp	80	10	6.8 −6.2	60	10	6.8 −4.6
subtotal e-commerce			−33.5			−10.1
Telework		million	kWh/yr		million	kWh/yr
number	28%	45.0		9%	15.0	
avg days per week	3			2		
electricity savings			−5,178 −233.0			−3,452 −51.8
subtotal ICT-driven			−243			81
subtotal non-ICT			1,646			1,646
Total commercial			1,403			1,727
EIA ICT			346			346
EIA non-ICT			1,494			1,494
EIA total commercial			1,840			1,840
difference from EIA						
TWH			−437			−113
%			−24			−6

[a]SP = savings potential.
[b]SC&L = space conditioning and lighting.

U.S. Industrial	2001 Base			2006		
industrial output (billion 1992$)			4,969			5,830
electricity intensity (kWh/$output)			0.21			0.20
Item	# units (million)	unit kWh/yr	TWh/yr	# units (million)	unit kWh/yr	TWh/yr
ICT equipment						
office equipment			12.7			14.0
production ICT equip			4.0			7.0
subtotal ICT equipment			16.7			21.0
Process control	% SP[a]	% pene-tration	drives % of elec	% SP[a]	% pene-tration	drives % of elec
adj speed motors	15	10.0	51 −7.8	17	20.0	50 −19.3
Building EMS	% SP[a]	% pene-tration	HVAC & lgt % of use	% SP[a]	% pene-tration	HVAC & lgt % of use
Phase1	6	10	16 −1.0	6	15	16 −1.6
Phase 2	16	1	16 −0.3	16	10	16 −2.9
Phase 3	24	0	16 0.0	24	5	16 −2.2
subtotal EMS			−1.2			−6.7
E-commerce	% online	% inven saved	intensity (kWh/$)	% online	% inven saved	intensity (kWh/$)
inventory savings	5	10	0.21 −1.1	20	15	0.20 −6.9
Telework		million	kWh/yr		million	kWh/yr
number	9%	4.3		13%	6.3	
avg days/week	2			2.1		
electricity savings			−3,034 −12.9			−3,300 −20.6
subtotal ICT-driven			−6			−33
subtotal non-ICT			1,029			1,141
Total industrial			1,023			1,108
EIA total industrial			1,023			1,134
difference from EIA						
TWh			0			−26
%			0			−2

References and data sources
EIA, 2001
Kawamoto et al., 2001
Roth, Goldstein, and Kleinman, 2002
MECS, 1998

[a]SP = savings potential.

U.S. Industrial	Reference 2021			Zaibatsu 2021		
industrial output (billion 1992$)			8,667			8,667
electricity intensity (kWh/$output)			0.14			0.15
Item	**# units (million)**	**unit kWh/yr**	**TWh/yr**	**# units (million)**	**unit kWh/yr**	**TWh/yr**
office equipment			19.0			21.0
production ICT equip			16.0			17.0
subtotal ICT equipment			35.0			38.0

Process control	% SP[a]	% pene- tration	drives % of elec		% SP[a]	% pene- tration	drives % of elec	
adj speed motors	20	40.0	49	−56.3	20	45.0	49	−63.3

Building EMS	% SP[a]	% pene- tration	HVAC & lgt % of use		% SP[a]	% pene- tration	HVAC & lgt % of use	
phase 1	6	20	15	−2.6	6	20	15	−2.6
phase 2	16	20	15	−6.9	16	20	15	−6.9
phase 3	24	25	15	−12.9	24	30	15	−15.5
subtotal EMS				−22.4				−25.0

E-commerce	% online	% inven saved	intensity (kwh/$)		% online	% inven saved	intensity (kwh/$)	
inventory savings	70	20	0.14	−34.3	75	25	0.15	−49.2

Telework		million					million	
number	18%	10.0			14%		7.5	
avg days /week	2.5				2			
electricity savings			−4,315	−43.2			−3,452	−25.9

subtotal ICT-driven				−121				−125
subtotal non-ICT				1,445				1,448
Total industrial				1,324				1,323
EIA total industrial				1,436				1,436
difference from EIA								
TWh				−112				−113
%				−8				−8

[a]SP = savings potential.

U.S. Industrial	Cybertopia 2021				Net Insecurity 2021			
				8,667				8,667
				0.12				0.14
Item	# units (million)	unit kWh/yr		TWh/yr	# units (million)	unit kWh/yr		TWh/yr
office equipment				20.0				19.0
production ICT equip				18.0				16.0
subtotal ICT equipment				38.0				35.0
Process control	% SP[a]	% penetration	drives % of elec		% SP[a]	% penetration	drives % of elec	
adj speed motors	20	50.0	49	−70.4	20	40.0	49	−56.3
Building EMS	% SP[a]	% penetration	HVAC & lgt % of use		% SP[a]	% penetration	HVAC & lgt % of use	
phase 1	6	20	15	−2.6	6	15	15	−1.9
phase 2	16	25	15	−8.6	16	20	15	−6.9
phase 3	24	35	15	−18.1	24	25	15	−12.9
subtotal EMS				−29.3				−21.8
E-commerce	% online	% inven saved	intensity (kWh/$)		% online	% inven saved	intensity (kWh/$)	
inventory savings	80	35	0.12	−58.8	60	20	0.14	−29.4
Telework		million	kWh/yr			million	kWh/yr	
number	28%	15.0			9%	5.0		
avg days per week	3				2			
electricity savings			−5,178	−77.7			−3,452	−17.3
subtotal ICT-driven				−198				−90
subtotal non-ICT				1,448				1,448
Total industrial				1,250				1,358
EIA total industrial				1,436				1,436
difference from EIA								
TWh				−186				−78
%				−13				−5

[a]SP = savings potential.

Total:			TWh/yr			
			Reference	Zaibatsu	Cyber-topia	Net Insecurity
	2001	2006	2021	2021	2021	2021
Residential + Commercial + Industrial						
Computer, office, network equipment	118	148	222	246	199	261
Other ICT equipment	79	98	184	190	193	206
Process controls	−8	−19	−56	−63	−70	−56
Building EMS	−5	−40	−152	−171	−216	−124
E-commerce	−3	−14	−55	−75	−92	−40
Telework	−32	−53	−120	−72	−216	−48
Subtotal ICT-driven	150	119	22	55	−203	200
Subtotal non-ICT	3,273	3,635	4,608	4,610	4,610	4,610
Total	3,423	3,755	4,630	4,665	4,407	4,810
EIA total	3,423	3,844	4,976	4,976	4,976	4,976
difference from EIA						
TWh	0	−89	−346	−311	−569	−166
%	0	−2	−7	−6	−11	−3

Aebischer, Bernard, and Alois Huser (2000), *Networking in Private Households—Impacts on Electricity Consumption*, Report on Behalf of the Swiss Federal Office of Energy, CEPE/ETHZ/ Encontrol, November.

Agre, Philip, "Red Rock Eater News Service," http://dlis.gseis.ucla. edu/people/pagre/rre.html (last accessed August 30, 2002).

Ainsworth, Diane (2001), "'Smart' Sensor Technologies Promise Big Savings in State Energy Costs," *Berkeleyan*, May 25.

Air University (1995), *Air Force 2025*, http://www.au.af.mil/au/2025/ index2.htm (last accessed August 30, 2002).

Alderfer, R. Brent, M. Monika Eldridge, and Thomas J. Starrs (2000), "Making Connections: Case Studies of Interconnection Barriers and Their Impact on Distributed Power Projects," National Renewable Energy Laboratory, NREL/SR-200-28053, May.

Allenby, Brad, and Darian Unger (2001), "Information Technology Impacts on the U.S. Energy Demand Profile," in *E-Vision 2000, Key Issues That Will Shape Our Energy Future: Analyses and Papers Prepared for the E-Vision 2000 Conference*, Santa Monica, CA: RAND, CF-170/1-1-DOE.

Amin, Massoud (2001), "Toward Self-Healing Energy Infrastructure Systems," *IEEE Computer Applications in Power*, January, pp. 20–28.

Amin, Massoud (1999), "National Infrastructures as Complex Interactive Networks," in Samad and Weyrauch, eds., *Automation, Control and Complexity: New developments and Directions*, New York: John Wiley & Sons.

Anderson, Robert H., P.S. Anton, Steven C. Bankes, Tora K. Bikson, Jonathan P. Caulkins, Peter J. Denning, James A. Dewar, Richard O. Hundley, and C.R. Neu (2000), *The Global Course of the Information Revolution: Technological Trends*, Santa Monica, CA: RAND, CF-157-NIC.

Arrington, Christine (2001), "Will Confusion Slow Home Networking?" *Media Device Report*, Mill Valley, CA: Jon Peddie Associates, May 14.

Aubin, C., D. Fougere, E. Husson, and M. Ivaldi (1995), "Real-Time Pricing of Electricity for Residential Customers: Econometric Analysis of an Experiment," *Journal of Applied Econometrics*, 10, pp. S171–S191.

Balkovich, Edward E., and Robert H. Anderson (2001), "Critical Infrastructures Will Remain Vulnerable: Neighborhoods Must Fend for Themselves," Alexandria, VA: Workshop on Mitigating the Vulnerability of Critical Infrastructures to Catastrophic Failure, September 10–11.

Borbely, Anne-Marie (2000), "How Good Is Your Power? Electronic Equipment Makes Heightened Sensitivity to Power Quality an Asset," *Energy User News*, September, pp. 13–15.

Botterman, Maarten, Robert H. Anderson, Paul van Binst, Martin Libicki, Andreas Ligtvoet, Robbin te Velde, and Gert Jan de Vries (2001), "Enabling the Information Society by Stimulating the Creation of a Broadband Environment in Europe: Analyses of Evolution Scenarios for Future Networking Technologies and Networks in Europe," draft report, Leiden, The Netherlands, and Brussels, Belgium: RAND Europe and Université Libre de Bruxelles, November.

Brock, Jon T. (2001), "Puget Sound Energy and Schlumberger RMS Partner to Provide Nation's Largest Networked Time-of-Day Rate

Program," Scientech Issue Alert, April 30, http://secure.scientech.com/issuealert/article.asp?id=704 (last accessed August 30, 2002).

Brynjolfsson, Erik, and Brian Kahin (2000), eds., *Understanding the Digital Economy*, Cambridge, MA: MIT Press.

Bureau of Economic Analysis (2001), "Table 5.12B. Private Inventories and Domestic Final Sales by Industry," *National Income and Product Accounts*, U.S. Department of Commerce, http://www.bea.doc.gov/bea/dn/nipaweb.

Bureau of Labor Statistics (1999), "Occupational Employment Statistics," U.S. Department of Labor, http://stats.bls.gov/oes/1999/oesi2_35.htm (last accessed August 30, 2002).

Clancy, Noreen, and David Rejeski, eds. (2001), *Our Future, Our Environment*, Santa Monica, CA: RAND, IP-207, http://www.rand.org/scitech/stpi/ourfuture (last accessed August 30, 2002).

Commercial Buildings Energy Consumption Survey [CBECS] (1995), "Summary Comparison Table," Energy Information Administration, U.S. Department of Energy, http://www.eia.doe.gov/emeu/consumptionbriefs/cbecs/pbawebsite/summarytable.htm (last accessed August 30, 2002).

Commission on Engineering and Technical Systems (1986), *Electricity in Economic Growth*, National Research Council, Washington, DC: National Academy Press, http://books.nap.edu/books/0309036771/html/116.html (last accessed August 30, 2002).

Computer Science and Telecommunications Board (2001a), *The Internet's Coming of Age*, National Research Council, Washington, DC: National Academy Press.

Computer Science and Telecommunications Board (2001b), *Broadband: Bringing Home the Bits*, National Research Council, Washington, DC: National Academy Press.

Computer Science and Telecommunications Board (1999), *Trust in Cyberspace*, National Research Council, Washington, DC: National Academy Press.

Computer Science and Telecommunications Board (1997), *The Evolution of Untethered Communications*, National Research Council, Washington, DC: National Academy Press.

Computer Science and Telecommunications Board (1996), *The Unpredictable Certainty*, National Research Council, Washington, DC: National Academy Press.

Computer Science and Telecommunications Board (1995), *Information Technology for Manufacturing*, National Research Council, Washington, DC: National Academy Press.

Computer Science and Telecommunications Board (1994), *Realizing the Information Future*, National Research Council, Washington, DC: National Academy Press.

Computer Science and Telecommunications Board (1988), *Toward a National Research Network*, National Research Council, Washington, DC: National Academy Press.

Consortium for Electric Infrastructure to Support a Digital Society [CEIDS] (2001a), *Value Assessment*, Palo Alto, CA: EPRI, July 10, p. 20.

Consortium for Electric Infrastructure to Support a Digital Society (2001b), "Draft R&D Plan," Palo Alto, CA: EPRI, April 4, http://ceids.epri.com/ceids/Docs/CEIDS_RD_Plan_040201.pdf (last accessed August 30, 2002).

Consortium for Electric Infrastructure for a Digital Society (2001c), *The Cost of Power Disturbances to Industrial and Digital Economy Companies*, Palo Alto, CA: EPRI, June 29.

Corcoran, Elizabeth (2001), "Too Hot to Handle," *Forbes*, April 20.

Cyberatlas, http://cyberatlas.internet.com (last accessed August 30, 2002).

Defense Advanced Research Projects Agency, "Palm Power," http://www.darpa.mil/dso/thrust/md/palmpower/program.html (last accessed August 30, 2002).

Dertouzos, Michael L. (1998), *What Will Be: How the New World of Information Will Change Our Lives*, New York: Harper.

Dewar, James A. (2002), *Assumption-Based Planning: A Tool for Reducing Avoidable Surprises*, Cambridge, UK: Cambridge University Press, in press.

Douglas, John (2000), "Power for a Digital Society," *EPRI Journal*, Winter, pp. 18–25.

Douglas, John (1999), "Power Delivery in the 21st Century," *EPRI Journal*, Summer, pp. 20–25.

Ducatel, Ken, Juliet Webster, and Werner Herrmann (2000), eds., *The Information Society in Europe: Work and Life in an Age of Globalization*, Lanham, MD: Rowman and Littlefield.

Dunn, Seth (2001), *Micropower: The Next Electrical Era*, Worldwatch Institute, http://www.worldwatch.org/pubs/paper151.html (last accessed August 30, 2002).

eMarketer, http://www.emarketer.com (last accessed August 30, 2002).

Energy Information Administration [EIA] (2001), *Annual Energy Outlook 2002 with Projections to 2020 [AEO 2002]*, Washington, DC: U.S. Department of Energy, DOE/EIA-0383, December.

Energy Information Administration (1999), "Inventory of Electric Utility Power Plants in the United States 1999," http://www.eia.doe.gov/cneaf/electricity/ipp/ipp99_sum.html (last accessed August 30, 2002).

Energy Information Administration (1998a), *1998 Manufacturing Energy Consumption Survey [MECS 1998]*, "Electricity: Components of Net Demand, 1998," Table N13.1, U.S. Department of Energy, http://www.eia.doe.gov/emeu/mecs/mecs98/datatables/d98n13_1.htm (last accessed August 30, 2002).

Energy Information Administration (1998b), *1998 Manufacturing Energy Consumption Survey [MECS 1998]*, "Number of Establishments by Participation in Energy-Management Activity, 1998," Table C9.1, U.S. Department of Energy, http://www.eia.doe.gov/emeu/mecs/mecs98/datatables/d98c9_1.htm (last accessed August 30, 2002).

EnerVision (1998), "The Introduction of Real Time Pricing," *The Edge*, Winter, http://www.enervision-inc.com (last accessed August 30, 2002).

EPRI (2001), "Stanford Workshop Updates Real-Time Pricing Outlook," *EPRI Journal Online*, http://www.epri.com/journal/details.asp?id=174&doctype=features (last accessed August 30, 2002).

EPRI (1999a), "Electricity Technology Roadmap: 1999 Summary and Synthesis Report," July, http://www.epri.com/corporate/discover_epri/roadmap/index.html (last accessed August 30, 2002).

EPRI (1999b), "AEP and Siemens Team to Develop Country's First Premium Power Park," press release, August 19, http://www.epri.com/corporate/discover_epri/news/releases/powerpark.html (last accessed August 30, 2002).

Fairley, Peter (2001), "A Smarter Power Grid," *Technology Review*, July/August, pp. 41–49.

Forrester Research (2002), "Forrester Online Retail Index," http://www.forrester.com/NRF/1,2873,0,00.html (last accessed August 30, 2002).

Gates, Bill, Nathan Myhrvold, and Peter M. Rinearson (1996), *The Road Ahead*, New York: Penguin USA.

Glenn, Jerome C., and Theodore J. Gordon (2000), *State of the Future at the Millennium*, AC/UNU Millennium Project, http://www.geocities.com/CapitolHill/Senate/4787/millennium/issues.html (last accessed August 30, 2002).

Groot, M.I., and P.J.S. Siderius (2000), *Monitors Statistical Analysis On-Mode Power Consumption*, report prepared by Van Holsteijn en Kemna BV on behalf of Novem BV, 6130 AA Sitard, The Netherlands, April.

Gyuk, Imre (2000), "Power Delivery in a Digital World," paper presented at the Electric Energy Storage and Technology Conference, Orlando, FL, September 18–20.

Hawken, Paul, Amory Lovins, and L. Hunter Lovins (1999), *Natural Capitalism*, Boston, MA: Little, Brown and Company.

Hayes, Brian (2001), "The Computer and the Dynamo," *American Scientist* 89, pp. 390–394.

Huber, Peter (2000), "More Kilowatts, Please," *Forbes*, November 27.

Huber, Peter, and Mark Mills (2001), "The National Energy Policy Development Plan: A Technology Investment Perspective," *The Huber/Mills Digital Power Report*, Guilder Publishing, LLC.

Huber, Peter, and Mark Mills (1999), "Dig More Coal—The PCs Are Coming," *Forbes*, May 31, pp. 71–72.

Hundley, Richard O., Robert H. Anderson, Tora K. Bikson, James A. Dewar, Jerrold D. Green, Martin Libicki, and C.R. Neu (2000), *The Global Course of the Information Revolution: Political, Economic and Social Consequences*, Santa Monica, CA: RAND, CF-154-NIC.

IBM (2001), "IBM Unveils Revolutionary Low-Power Chip Technologies," press release, October 12, http://www.ibm.com/news/us/2001/10/12.html (last accessed August 30, 2002).

Info-Communications Development Authority of Singapore (2000), "Infocomm Technology Roadmap (Broadband Access and Mobile Wireless)," http://www.ida.gov.sg/Website/IDAhome.nsf/Home?OpenForm (last accessed August 30, 2002).

Information Society Technologies Advisory Group (2001), *Scenarios for Ambient Intelligence in 2010*, http://www.cordis.lu/ist/istag.htm (last accessed August 30, 2002).

Information Technology Industry Council (n.d.), "ITI (CBEMA) Curve Application Note," http://www.itic.org/technical/iticurv.pdf (last accessed August 30, 2002).

Interlaboratory Working Group (2000), *Scenarios for a Clean Energy Future*, Oak Ridge, TN, and Berkeley, CA: Oak Ridge National Laboratory and Lawrence Berkeley National Laboratory, ORNL/CON-476 and LBNL-44029, November.

JALA International, Inc. (1998), "Telework Center Cost-Benefit Analysis," http://www.jala.com/twctrcba.htm (last accessed August 30, 2002).

Jorgenson, Dale W., and Kevin J. Stiroh (2001), "Raising the Speed Limit: Economic Growth in the Information Age," in *E-Vision 2000, Key Issues That Will Shape Our Energy Future: Analyses and Papers Prepared for the E-Vision 2000 Conference*, Santa Monica, CA: RAND, CF-170/1-1-DOE.

Kahan, Brian, ed. (1993), *Building Information Infrastructure*, New York: McGraw-Hill Primis.

Kawamoto, Kaoru, Jonathan G. Koomey, Bruce Nordman, Richard E. Brown, Maryann Piette, Michael Ting, and Alan K. Meier (2001), *Electricity Used by Office Equipment and Network Equipment in the U.S.*, Berkeley, CA: Lawrence Berkeley National Laboratory, LBNL-45917.

Koomey, Jonathan G. (2000), "Rebuttal to Testimony on 'Kyoto and the Internet: The Energy Implications of the Digital Economy,'" Lawrence Berkeley National Laboratory, LBNL-46509, August.

Koomey, Jonathan, Kaoru Kawamoto, Bruce Nordman, Mary Ann Piette, and Richard E. Brown, (1999), "Initial Comments on 'The Internet Begins with Coal,'" Lawrence Berkeley National Laboratory, LBNL-44698, December.

Kurzweil, Ray (1998), *The Age of Spiritual Machines: When Computers Exceed Human Intelligence*, New York: Viking.

Lessig, Lawrence (1999), *Code, and Other Laws of Cyberspace*, New York: Basic Books.

Lewis, Rosalind (2000), *Information Technology in the Home: Barriers, Opportunities, and Research Directions*, Santa Monica, CA: RAND, IP-203-OSTP.

Margeherio, Lynn, David Henry, Sandra Cooke, and Sabrina Montes (1998), *The Emerging Digital Economy*, Washington, DC: Economics and Statistics Administration, Office of Policy Development, U.S. Department of Commerce, April, http://www.esa.doc.

gov/508/esa/TheEmergingDigitalEconomy.htm (last accessed August 30, 2002).

Martino, Joseph P. (1978), *Technological Forecasting for Decision-making*, New York: Elsevier.

Mills, Mark P. (1999), "The Internet Begins with Coal: A Preliminary Exploration of the Impact of the Internet on Electricity Consumption," Arlington, VA: The Greening Earth Society, May.

Mitchell, William J. (1997), *City of Bits: Space, Place, and the Infobahn*, Cambridge, MA: MIT Press.

Mitchell-Jackson, Jennifer D. (2001), *Energy Needs in an Internet Economy: A Closer Look at Data Centers*, Master's thesis, University of California at Berkeley, http://enduse.lbl.gov/Info/datacenterreport.pdf (last accessed August 30, 2002).

Mitchell-Jackson, Jennifer, Jonathan G. Koomey, Bruce Nordman, and Michele Blazek (2001), *Data Center Power Requirements: Measurements from Silicon Valley*, Berkeley, CA: Lawrence Berkeley National Laboratory, LBNL-48554, July.

Mokhtarian, Patricia L. (1998), "A Synthetic Approach to Estimating the Impacts of Telecommuting on Travel," *Urban Studies*, 35(2), pp. 215–248.

National Institute of Standards and Technology (1994), "Supply and Demand of Electric Power and the NII," draft for comment, Washington, DC: National Institute of Standards and Technology, September 7.

National Intelligence Council (2000), *Global Trends 2015*, http://www.cia.gov/cia/publications/globaltrends2015 (last accessed August 30, 2002).

Negroponte, Nicholas (1995), *Being Digital*, New York: Knopf.

Nilles, Jack M. (2000), *Telework in the U.S.: Telework America Survey 2000*, Washington, DC: International Telework Association and Council.

Nilles, Jack M. (1998), *Managing Telework*, New York: John Wiley & Sons.

Norford, L., A. Hatcher, J. Harris, J. Roturier, and O. Yu (1990), "Electricity Use in Information Technologies," *Annual Review of Energy*, pp. 423–453.

Norman, Donald A. (1998), The Invisible Computer, Cambridge, MA: MIT Press.

OECD (1999), *The Economic and Social Impacts of Electronic Commerce: Preliminary Findings and Research Agenda*, Paris, France: Organisation for Economic Co-operation and Development, http://www.oecd.org/pdf/M00032000/M00032941.pdf (last accessed August 30, 2002).

Office of Power Technologies (2000), "Strategic Plan," Energy Efficiency and Renewable Energy, U.S. Department of Energy, October, http://www.eren.doe.gov/power/pdfs/opt_strategic_plan.pdf (last accessed August 30, 2002).

Park, Andrew (2000), "Powering the Internet," *Austin American-Statesman*, December 11.

Pew Internet and American Life Project (2002), *The Broadband Difference: How Online Americans' Behavior Changes with High-Speed Internet Connections at Home*, June 23, http://www.pewinternet.org (last accessed August 30, 2002).

Pool, Ithiel de Sola (1983), *Forecasting the Telephone: A Retrospective Technology Assessment of the Telephone*, Norwood, NJ: Ablex.

President's Commission on Critical Infrastructure Protection (1997), *Critical Foundations: Protecting America's Infrastructures*, Washington, DC, October.

Rabaey, J., E. Arens, C. Federspiel, A. Gadgil, D. Messerschmitt, W. Nazaroff, K. Pister, S. Oren, and P. Varaiya (2001), *Smart Energy Distribution and Consumption: Information Technology as an Enabling Force*, University of California at Berkeley, Center for Information Technology Research in the Interest of Society, http://www.citris.berkeley.edu/SmartEnergy/SmartEnergy.html (last accessed August 30, 2002).

Reed, William L. (2001), "Competitive Electricity Markets and Innovative Technologies: Hourly Pricing Can Pave the Way for the

Introduction of Technology and Innovation," in *E-Vision 2000, Key Issues That Will Shape Our Energy Future: Analyses and Papers Prepared for the E-Vision 2000 Conference*, Santa Monica, CA: RAND, CF-170/1-1-DOE.

Robinson, Glenn O., ed. (1978), *Communications for Tomorrow*, New York: Praeger.

Rogers, Everett (1986), "Adoption and Implementation of Communication Technologies," *Communication Technology*, pp. 116–149.

Romm, Joseph (1999), *The Internet Economy and Global Warming*, The Center for Energy and Climate Solutions, December.

Rosen, Karen B., and Alan K. Meier (2000), *Energy Use of Home Audio Products in the U.S.*, Berkeley, CA: Lawrence Berkeley National Laboratory, LBNL-43468.

Rosen, Karen B., and Alan K. Meier (1999), *Energy Use of Televisions and Videocassette Recorders in the U.S.*, Berkeley, CA: Lawrence Berkeley National Laboratory, LBNL-42393.

Rosen, Karen B., Alan K. Meier, and Stephan Zandelin (2001), *Energy Use of Set-Top Boxes and Telephony Products in the U.S.*, Berkeley, CA: Lawrence Berkeley National Laboratory, LBNL-45305.

Roth, Kurt W., Fred Goldstein, and Jonathan Kleinman (2002), *Energy Consumption by Office and Telecommunications Equipment in Commercial Buildings—Volume I: Energy Consumption Baseline*, Cambridge, MA: Arthur D. Little, Inc., 72895-00, January, http://www.eren.doe.gov/buildings/documents/pdfs/office_telecom-vol1_final.pdf (last accessed August 30, 2002).

Sanchez, M.C., J.G. Koomey, M.M. Moezzi, A. Meier, and W. Huber (1998), "Miscellaneous Electricity in U.S. Homes: Historical Decomposition and Future Trends," *Energy Policy*, 26(8), pp. 585–593.

Schwartz, Peter (1991), *The Art of the Long View*, New York: Doubleday.

Silberglitt, Richard, Emile Ettedgui, and Anders Hove (2002), *Strengthening the Grid: Effect of High Temperature Super-*

conducting Power Technologies on Reliability, Power Transfer Capacity, and Energy Use, Santa Monica, CA: RAND, MR-1531-DOE.

Silberman, Steve (2001), "Girding Up for the Power Grid," *WiredNews,* June 14, http://www.wired.com/news/print/0,1294,44516,00.html (last accessed August 30, 2002).

Smil, Vaclev (2000), "Perils of Long-Range Forecasting: Reflections on Looking Far Ahead," *Technological Forecasting and Social Change,* 65, pp. 251–264.

SoftSwitching Technologies (n.d.), "Power-Related Downtime Costs $120-190 Billion Annually," http://www.softswitch.com/downtime.htm (last accessed August 30, 2002).

Standage, Tom (2001), "The Internet, Untethered," *The Economist,* October 11.

Templin, Neal (2001), "Power Hungry Web 'Server Farms' Find Cooler Reception In California," *The Wall Street Journal,* February 28.

UCLA Center for Communication Policy (2001), *The UCLA Internet Report 2001—Surveying the Digital Future,* November, http://www.ccp.ucla.edu/pages/internet-report.asp (last accessed August 30, 2002).

U.S. Census Bureau (2001a), "Population Projections," *Profiles and Demographic Characteristics, 2000 Census of Population and Housing,* U.S. Department of Commerce, http://www.census.gov/population/www/projections/popproj.html (last accessed August 30, 2002).

U.S. Census Bureau (2001b), "Labor Force, Employment and Earnings," U.S. Department of Commerce, http://www.census.gov/prod/2001pubs/statab/sec13.pdf (last accessed August 30, 2002).

U.S. Department of Commerce (2000), *Digital Economy 2000,* Washington, DC: Economics and Statistics Administration, Office of Policy Development, June, http://www.esa.doc.gov/de2k2.htm (last accessed August 30, 2002).

Van der Heijden, Kees (1996), *Scenarios: The Art of Strategic Conversation*, New York: Wiley.

Wack, Pierre (1985a), "Scenarios: Shooting the Rapids," *Harvard Business Review*, November/December, pp. 139–150.

Wack, Pierre (1985b), "Scenarios: Uncharted Waters Ahead," *Harvard Business Review*, September/October, pp. 73–89.

Waggoner, John (2000), "Power Quality and Harmonics," *Energy User News*, February 26.

Ware, Willis (1998), *The Cyber-Posture of the National Information Infrastructure*, Santa Monica, CA: RAND, MR-976-OSTP.

Working Group Forum on Critical Infrastructure Protection (2001), "An Approach to Action for the Electricity Sector," North American Electric Reliability Council, June, ftp://www.nerc.com/pub/sys/all_updl/cip/ApproachforAction_June2001.pdf (last accessed August 30, 2002).